Innovation

PACT

The No-Nonsense Guide to
Sustainable Innovation

Tim Howell

Published by made4gov

PO Box 820248, Houston, TX

★★★

★★★

ISBN: **0996270701**

ISBN-13: **978-0-9962707-0-0**

Library of Congress Control Number: 2015907165

LCCN Imprint Name: **made4gov, Houston TX**

Innovation PACT

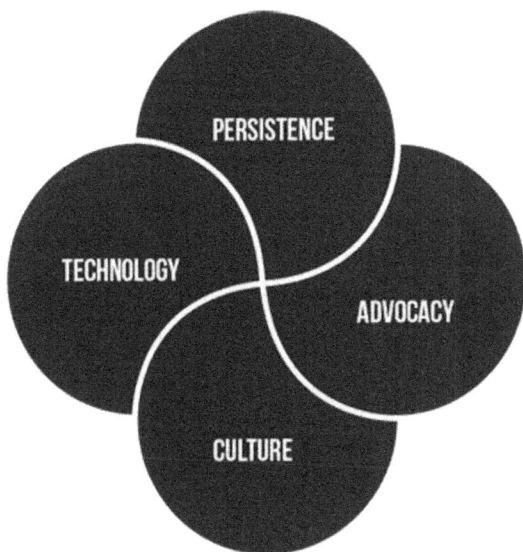

For more information, visit:

www.InnovationPACT.com

About This Book

Knowledge is important, but what we do with that knowledge is exponentially more important. I have studied and practiced innovation as part of my job and as an interest and passion for nearly a decade. During that time, I was able to help a number of government organizations become more innovative, but I knew there was more that I could do. This was the driving force behind writing this book.

There is a vast amount of information available on innovation online and in books, but none of these resources breaks the process down into actionable steps. Given that, I took the opposite approach, focusing primarily on action and eliminating most of the theories and studies. I did this knowing that I would put myself in the line of fire. There is no one way to do anything, and thus, others may not agree with my approach to creating an Innovation Strategy. I am OK with that.

The problem this book sets out to solve is not the same as that of other innovation books. Instead, this book is intended to be a guide that any organization can use to promote innovation. I wanted to make it so simple that you could read the entire book and begin creating your strategy in a few hours.

This book is broken down into six manageable sections:

Section 1: Laying the Foundation

Covers the basic concepts that all innovation leaders must understand before implementing an Innovation Strategy.

Section 2: Take the Innovation PACT

Examines in detail the Innovation PACT (Persistence, Accountability, Culture, and Technology).

Section 3: Innovation Strategy Components

Looks at the components that constitute an Innovation Strategy and information on how to complete each of those components in detail.

Section 4: Creating an Innovation Program

Covers the steps of an Innovation Program and provides tips for making it successful.

Section 5: Implementing Your Innovation Strategy

Offers a step-by-step guide to implementing an Innovation Strategy, walking you through everything covered in Sections 3 and 4.

Section 6: Maintaining Your Innovation Strategy

Examines the ongoing maintenance required to keep your Innovation Strategy up-to-date and moving forward.

You will also have access to a wealth of resources found at the accompanying website: www.InnovationPACT.com. This is a starting place for organizations looking to reap the benefits of becoming more innovative. I hope you find this book helpful and would love to hear from you. You can get in touch with me by visiting the Innovation PACT website. I want you to be successful, and wish you the best on your journey toward becoming more innovative.

Table of Contents

Innovation is not thinking outside of the box…It is the process of stretching the box from which our thoughts are constrained.

~Tim Howell

Introduction

We are about to embark on a journey—a journey that could dramatically transform your organization through the power of sustained innovation, a journey that will answer many of the questions you have about innovation. What is innovation exactly? How do we implement it? How do we measure it? And, most importantly, how do we sustain it?

These questions come up frequently, but few people know what the answers are. We see great ideas and innovative companies come and go, but we typically think of them as one-offs or as products of exceptional people who have some innate talent that we don't. Fortunately, that is not the case.

Organizations, like individuals, have to develop skills and create an environment where innovation can flourish. This requires that we first understand it. Unfortunately, most of the research on innovation focuses on disruptive innovation. It is easy to see why this is so, since it's this type of innovation that disrupts entire industries and changes the world.

I will take a different approach. Organizations and start-ups that are highly innovative naturally produce disruptive innovation, but it is not because of something they have figured out and we haven't. It is because they have the culture in place and the tenacity to make that innovation happen.

We will look at innovation from the ground up because that is where it starts. By making small changes and removing roadblocks, our organizations can become innovation-producing machines. That is the difference between highly innovative companies and other companies. Highly innovative companies work hard to create an environment where innovation can flourish, and they do not give up when things get difficult.

This journey will provide you with all of the necessary steps to become a highly innovative company. It will help prevent the status-quo mentality that sets in when bureaucracy, policies, procedures, and other roadblocks get in the way. By taking a step back and focusing on the big picture, you can make substantial changes. It is time to realize that all organizations can be more innovative—if they make the effort. I will show you how to make this happen.

So What Makes This Book Different?

Countless books have been written on the science of innovation and the role it plays in the world. This is not one of those books. Those books are filled with research, studies, and examples of innovation. They are great books, and I have read many of them. The problem is that they don't focus on how to put those concepts into action.

Innovation PACT will walk you through the basics of innovation and provide you with the resources necessary to take the next steps. We will not get caught up in the science or spend time hashing out theories or hypotheses. Instead, we will focus on the fundamentals of innovation, how to create an Innovation Strategy, and how to implement an Innovation Program. Doing these things will lead to increased innovation and, more important, sustainable innovation. Whether you are a nonprofit, a private company, or a public entity, you can benefit from being more innovative.

I congratulate you for taking the first step. After reading *Innovation PACT*, you should have everything you need to get started. This book will be your innovation handbook, and the resources provided will jump-start your Innovation Strategy and make it easy to begin. Put in the time it takes to read this book, and then keep it handy as a reference guide.

Innovation Strategy

Organizations talk a lot about strategy, but few consider an Innovation Strategy. *Innovation PACT* provides the resources and knowledge an organization needs to create and implement an Innovation Strategy. In my experience, this is the best way to set up an organization for the highest likelihood of producing sustainable innovation.

Innovation is like many other leadership undertakings: it takes planning and has to be aligned with many areas of an organization. Your Innovation Strategy will tie in to your overall strategy, and your resources will have to be allocated to make it successful. Doing it right in the beginning will help eliminate roadblocks and provide the best return on your time and investment.

We will take a more detailed look at what's included in your Innovation Strategy in Section 3. For now, it is important to understand that creating your Innovation Strategy is the ultimate goal of this book. The strategy will be a simplified approach to how your organization promotes innovation.

I hope you are as excited as I am about the opportunities that having an Innovation Strategy in place can present. I have seen many organizations do the things outlined in this book with great results. You will have the opportunity to re-create what they have done and apply it to your organization.

The Purpose of This Book

As you make your way through *Innovation PACT*, you will quickly see that the information provided is specifically geared toward getting you started with your first Innovation Strategy. The purpose of this strategy is to fulfill the requirements of adopting the Innovation PACT, which is key to creating sustainable innovation inside your organization.

This book was carefully crafted with that aspiration in mind. By approaching the book in this manner, I was able to create a no-nonsense guide that you can read in a few hours.

But do not let the length fool you. The value you can get out of completing the steps in this book has no direct correlation with the number of pages. In fact, the simplicity of the text makes the book extremely actionable and limits the barriers to getting started.

However, there is a caveat. To achieve the objective of simplicity, I had to be very selective about what I included. Nonetheless, we live in a time in which information is digital. The knowledge you gain herein does not have to stop when the pages run out. You also have the Innovation PACT website (http://www.InnovationPACT.com) to support you.

In reality, *Innovation PACT* is just a starting point. The work you do inside your organization and the ever-growing body of information available on the website will pick up where the book leaves off. That is why I encourage you to check out the website, download its resources, and subscribe to the Innovation PACT newsletter to continue your journey.

Once you have invested your time and money in the Innovation PACT, you can reap the benefits of a community of innovators and innovative organizations. I am passionate about innovation and enjoy learning about it through my own experiences and the experiences of others. I also enjoy writing about what I have learned. Therefore, you will have access to my passion and knowledge, filtered into manageable chunks of valuable information beyond these pages.

Resources

You are not alone on this journey. As you make your way through this book, you will see additional information on available resources. This is where the website http://www.InnovationPACT.com comes in. You will find helpful resources there and other important information that pertains to this book. These resources are not required to get value out of this book, but the goal is to provide you with everything you need to make innovation a success in your organization.

Please take the time to read through *Innovation PACT* before trying to move forward. Having a basic understanding in place will be very important as you take this journey. I am excited for the opportunity you have to transform your organization. Let's get started!

Section 1

Laying the Foundation

Before we jump into the Innovation Strategy, there are a few important concepts every leader of innovation must understand. I will summarize them here so that we can quickly move through them. Please pay close attention, because understanding these concepts is crucial to the success of your Innovation Strategy.

Let's Clear Some Things Up

I will try to stay jargon-free and use as little "innovation speak" as possible. (I am a technology geek by trade, and my wife is an attorney, so between the two of us we could write our own language.) There are, however, a few words and phrases I will use that may not be exactly clear, so I will do my best to explain them here.

Innovation

Let's start with the word "innovation" itself. *Merriam-Webster* defines "innovation" as "the action or process of innovating." That is as clear as mud.

Now let's take a look at just the word "innovate." *Merriam-Webster* defines "innovate" as "making changes in something established, especially by introducing new methods, ideas, or products." That is getting closer, but I have my own definition:

Innovation is the introduction of new ways to handle situations or problems that provide a better result than the current methods.

Simply put, anytime you do something different (preferably better) than the way it is currently being done, you are being innovative. This could be through the introduction of new technology or via something as simple as modifying steps in a process.

If we break innovation down into its simplest form, it becomes easier to encourage and teach it. Under that definition, I could probably teach a cat to be more innovative, but let's hope our organizations are already more innovative than our feline friends. The goal here is to promote innovation that starts out small and builds over time. This will make it more sustainable while also limiting exposure to the inherent risks associated with change.

Ideation and Ideation System

There is no shortage of good ideas inside your organization. The point of Ideation and the Ideation System is to capture those ideas and make sure they are acted upon. Ironically, much of the innovation that takes place in companies does not get classified as an "idea." Someone is just working as usual, realizes there is an easier or better way, and just starts doing it. This happens all the time, even when organizations do everything they can to try to stop it. This is innovation at a very basic level.

Ideation is the process of conjuring up or formulating an idea. This is important in formal innovation where ideas are focused on a specific problem. The term is mostly used in the context of an Ideation System or Ideation software, but you will also see it used in other contexts when discussing innovation.

The Ideation System is the system that manages your formal Ideation initiative. Confusing? Perhaps, but we will explore ways to make it relatively simple. An Ideation System can be a manual process or managed by software. The system explains how ideas are collected, ranked, implemented, and rewarded. It will open the floodgate of good ideas inside your organization, so you have to be ready for it. That is why we will look at this in greater detail in Sections 3 and 4. Your Innovation Strategy will include an Ideation System, so understanding these terms is very important.

Innovation Strategy and Program

As with many leadership terms, there are often words or phrases that are not completely clear. "Innovation Program" and "Innovation Strategy" may seem similar, but they are not interchangeable.

The term "Innovation Strategy" is still relatively new and is not used often, although I hope we can change that together. When I refer to "Innovation Strategy," I am referring to the overall strategy that encompasses everything you are doing to help promote innovation. In contrast, when I refer to

"Innovation Program," I am talking about a focused initiative that aims to solve a specific challenge or problem.

You will have many Innovation Programs but only one Innovation Strategy. Examples of Innovation Programs might involve an effort to improve employee morale or increase sales on a certain product line. These will be specific initiatives to help solve Organizational Pain Points identified in your Innovation Strategy. These objectives are fairly focused but are still big enough to make a substantial impact in an organization. We will cover this in much more detail, but understanding how the two are different and how they relate is important when making your way through this book.

Organizations

I have worked for both private and public-sector companies, but most of my experience with innovation comes through working with local government agencies. However, the concepts in this book can apply to the private sector, public sector, and nonprofits. Therefore, I use the term "organization" interchangeably to represent any of these segments.

There are some obvious differences across all three segments, but when it comes to innovation, the concepts behind implementing a solid Innovation Strategy are the same. The techniques that have worked for companies have also worked for nonprofits and government agencies. Identify what your organization does well and what it needs to work on, and you will create a balanced strategy that is aligned with your overall goals.

How Innovation Works

Many individuals and universities have studied innovation in great detail. Over the past few years, much of this information has become widely available through books and articles. I am not qualified to discuss these topics in length.

However, I know enough to be able to identify the important topics that you should understand prior to implementing an Innovation Strategy. These points of focus will help you appreciate the process of innovation and determine how to best implement an Innovation Strategy inside your organization. They will equip you with the knowledge to know when innovation is working and how to modify the environment when it is not. Let's take a look at each in more detail.

Ideas Are Connected

If you look at history, innovation doesn't come just from giving people incentives; it comes from creating environments where ideas can connect.

—Steven Johnson

The concept that ideas are connected is extremely important to understand. Ideas do not materialize out of thin air, perfectly formulated, and ready to be served up. Instead, they are an accumulation of thoughts, concepts, interactions, and experiences that have been combined into an idea.

Mark Twain is quoted as saying:

> There is no such thing as a new idea. It is impossible. We simply take a lot of old ideas and put them into a sort of mental kaleidoscope. We give them a turn and they make new and curious combinations. We keep on turning and making new

combinations indefinitely; but they are the same old pieces of colored glass that have been in use through all the ages.

Mark Twain is spot on. His insights help us understand that ideas are connected. The more we allow ideas to connect and develop, the more ideas we will produce. These ideas might involve creating unstructured discussions, promoting more interactions through group work, or even updating the break room. Some of the most complex problems many organizations face do not get solved simply because ideas are not allowed to connect.

Adjacent Possible

I first came across the term "Adjacent Possible" in Steven Johnson's book, *Where Good Ideas Come From.* This is a very interesting concept that outlines how innovation progresses, while at the same time demonstrating its limitations. I will do my best to explain it here. Figure 1a helps illustrate this key concept.

Throughout history, large-scale innovation has been incremental. This is because early innovations had to be created to make future innovations possible. As each new innovation happened, it opened a door to new possibilities. This incremental approach both restricts and empowers innovation.

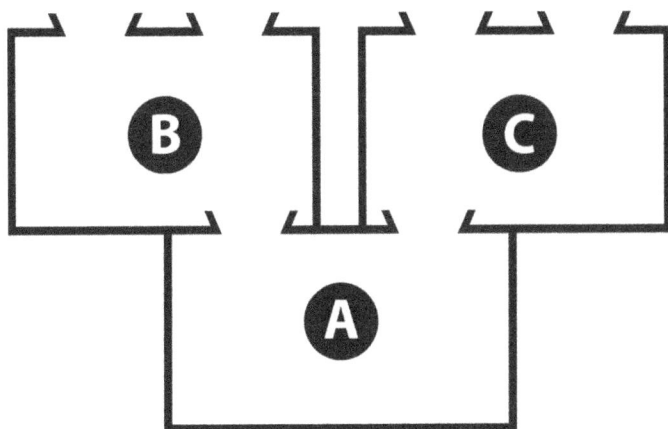

Figure 1a. Large-scale innovation happens in the Adjacent Possible by discovering one small idea (door) at a time.

Steven Johnson explains this as being like going into a magical house that automatically expands every time you open a new door. Each door in the current or previous room is within the Adjacent Possible, but you are not able to skip ahead a room without first exploring the connecting rooms. As you explore each room, new doors (possibilities) present themselves.

Large-scale innovation happens incrementally through the exploration of the Adjacent Possible. It follows a set structure that allows innovations from all over the world to connect and build on one another. The Adjacent Possible also governs innovation by placing restrictions on just how innovative a specific person or idea can be.

It does not matter how good your idea is. If it is not within the Adjacent Possible, it will not happen without first building the incremental steps. The easiest example to demonstrate this is the Internet. Before you could spy on your friends on Facebook or push a button to tell the world about how your day was, a lot of things had to be in place.

First, the computer had to be created, and then the Internet. Then computers had to become mainstream. Then someone had to develop the software, and so on. So if Mark Zuckerberg had been born twenty years earlier and wanted to create Facebook, it would not have been possible because it was outside of the Adjacent Possible.

Why is the Adjacent Possible important for your organization? It is important because organizations have to go through some of the same steps to become more innovative. An organization cannot go from a little innovation to being extremely innovative overnight, and innovation projects should not be so big that they cross multiple levels of the Adjacent Possible.

It is also important to note that every time a new innovation is implemented, it has the potential to open many other possibilities. This allows you to get full value out of your innovation efforts. So when you are thinking about implementing some big idea, make sure it is in your Adjacent Possible before spending a lot of time, money, and effort on it.

Types of Innovation

Not all innovation is created equal. You will see innovation commonly lumped into one bucket, but that is simply not the case. Innovation can come in many forms. Understanding the different types will allow you to decide what makes sense in a particular situation.

As with most things in leadership, there is no consensus on what the principal types of innovation are. Therefore, I had to create my own. In the spirit of creating an easy-to-remember system, I refer to these categories as the "four *C*s of innovation." While the names for each type of innovation do not really matter, it is important to understand the differences so that you can tailor your Innovation Strategy to achieve your desired outcome.

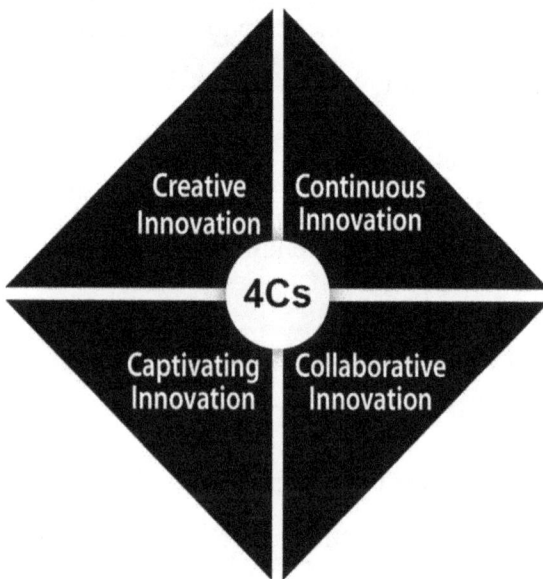

Figure 1b. The four Cs outline the four types of innovation.

The four *C*s of innovation are as follows:

- Creative Innovation
- Continuous Innovation

- Collaborative Innovation

- Captivating Innovation

Let's look at each one and examine the role it plays in your Innovation Strategy.

Creative Innovation

Creative Innovation involves individual innovation. It occurs when a talented individual, through his or her own effort, produces something innovative. This type of innovation is difficult to predict and teach, but there are some things leaders can do to create an environment that supports it.

Leadership must make knowledge available, provide skill-development opportunities, and give individuals the ability to make things happen in order to foster Creative Innovation. Let's take a look at these aspects in more detail.

Knowledge

Individuals must have access to knowledge, and leaders should do everything possible to make information available. This will help Creative Innovators fully understand the challenges the organization faces. If you have a well-informed employee base, you have a higher probability for Creative Innovation. That is because people must first understand the challenges in front of them before they can produce creative solutions.

Therefore, leadership should promote transparency and information sharing by emulating that behavior and breaking down silos within the organization. Leaders should also promote cross-departmental collaboration and shadowing.

Skills

Skills are important in innovation because they are often needed to execute an idea. This starts with identifying an individual's strengths and passions so that you can then provide the resources necessary to develop those skills. Training is often the missing puzzle piece between having a problem and knowing a solution.

Abilities

While having knowledge and capitalizing on skills are important, this is still not enough. Organizations must help their employees use their knowledge and skills to solve complex problems and make the organization more efficient.

Many roadblocks can stand in the way of innovation. The most common are ineffective leadership, bad policies, and lack of resources (such as time, tools, or capital). Leadership must identify and remove these barriers so that Creative Innovators can flourish.

Creative Innovators in the Innovation Strategy

Creative Innovation does not play a big role in your Innovation Strategy. Many of the things we talked about that enable Creative Innovators will be covered in other areas of the Innovation Strategy.

The reason we do not want to put a sharp focus on Creative Innovation is because it is much more difficult to sustain. Employees come and go, and if you depend on specific individuals for the innovation taking place within your organization, you will ultimately not be able to sustain it.

Let me emphasize that I am *not* saying that Creative Innovation is not important. It is important, and it is often the type of innovation that is the easiest to recognize. If you follow the tips outlined in Sections 2 and 3, you will naturally begin to enable Creative Innovators.

Continuous Innovation

Continuous Innovation involves business process improvement: when organizations evaluate and improve the way they operate. That makes it extremely important because every employee can get involved, and this has a compounding effect.

Continuous Innovation is usually introspective because it allows individuals to assess the status quo and then make minimal but effective improvements. Small changes to an environment can add up to huge wins over time. For example, removing a few steps from a business process or implementing a new tool to streamline part of a process may seem relatively insignificant, but the compounding effects can lead to profound transformations.

This concept is important because everything an organization does can on some level be broken down into a set of processes. Therefore, improving or eliminating steps in a process can be extremely valuable. This allows organizations to become more innovative over time with very little risk.

Continuous Innovation in the Innovation Strategy

Continuous Innovation will play a big role in your Innovation Strategy. This is the primary type of innovation you should focus on for overall organizational efficiency and effectiveness. Although Continuous Innovation is not as exciting as other types of innovation, it provides great value to an organization. It is also easier to sustain and can become contagious when it's ingrained in your organization's culture.

Collaborative Innovation

Collaborating across and outside of your organization can be a powerful tool for innovation. Collaborative Innovation starts with first identifying a problem or challenge, and then bringing the right people together to help solve it.

When we collaborate, we bring in people with various levels of education and experience in the hope of sparking a creative solution. Depending on your audience and the type of problems you are trying to solve, you will handle this in many different ways.

Internal collaboration usually involves creating teams or task forces to tackle a problem. It can also be accomplished through an Innovation Program. This is where you present a specific challenge and individuals come together to identify and discuss possible solutions.

External collaboration is similar to internal collaboration with one major difference: external collaboration takes your challenge and asks your external audience to help solve it. This could be customers if you are a business, supporters if you are a nonprofit, or the general public if you are a government agency.

The last type of collaboration is a hybrid approach: where you bring in people from within the organization alongside people from the external audience to help drive innovation. Usually, the external audience in this scenario is someone with specific experience in the area you are addressing.

Collaborative Innovation usually requires some type of formal collaboration software. By utilizing software, you make it easier to identify the resources required to implement a solution. This also makes it easier to keep the innovation effort focused and to deliver a solution that has buy-ins from a wide range of stakeholders.

Collaborative Innovation in the Innovation Strategy

Collaborative Innovation also plays a big role in your Innovation Strategy. Combined with Continuous Innovation, it will be the biggest focus area to create innovation that is both sustainable and provides value to the organization.

When you develop your Innovation Strategy, you will need to identify the system and processes for promoting Collaborative Innovation. This is where you will identify your Ideation System and the innovation team that will be responsible for providing the necessary resources and getting the right people involved.

Collaborative Innovation is the area that will take the most up-front work and planning, but it will also provide some of the biggest impacts, as this is where entire processes are eliminated or replaced. The results of Collaborative

Innovation have produced some great innovations, and I have no doubt that it will do the same for your organization.

Captivating Innovation

Every so often there is an innovation so great and disruptive that it changes the entire landscape. Innovations such as the iPad, electric cars, the World Wide Web, 3-D printers, and Craigslist are extreme examples of this. This is Captivating Innovation, which is commonly referred to as "disruptive innovation."

In most organizations this would be a new product or program that is substantially different from what was done in the past. This can cause organizations to completely shift their focus and resources, and usually results in emulation by other organizations. Captivating Innovation does not happen very often, but when it does, everybody notices.

Captivating Innovation in the Innovation Strategy

There is no secret formula for producing Captivating Innovation. Some companies have been able to produce it regularly, but when others try to emulate this, there is often little success. Therefore, Captivating Innovation is not covered in the Innovation Strategy.

However, that does not mean you should write it off. If you implement the Innovation Strategy components outlined in this book, you will be creating an environment that promotes Captivating Innovation.

As you roll out your Innovation Programs, keep an eye out for ideas that have the potential to produce Captivating Innovation. They may not always be the most popular, because this type of innovation can be hard to comprehend and sometimes even controversial.

Captivating Innovation can produce huge value, but you cannot force it. Focus on Continuous Innovation and Collaborative Innovation to set up your organization with the best possible chance for success.

Defining Your Audience

Identifying your audience is one of the first steps to putting together an Innovation Program. We can utilize many channels to drive innovation: internal employees, the leadership team, or even customers who use the products or services that you create. You need to look at the problem you are trying to solve and decide who should be involved in helping you solve it. To make things simple, we will split the audience into two categories: internal and external.

The internal audience usually represents your employees, leadership team, and the partners you work with. The external audience usually represents your customers, onlookers, or the governing body. You do not have any authority over this audience, but they can still be utilized to make sure your organization is heading in the right direction and meeting the needs of its customers.

The internal and external audiences are both important, but it is key that you identify which audience you are targeting with a specific Innovation Program. It is also important that you think about all audiences when creating your Innovation Strategy, as they will have a significant impact on your overall success.

Wrap-Up

If you have made it this far and understand most of the concepts discussed, go ahead and add innovation to your list of competencies. You now know more about innovation than the average leader. This information will be valuable as you begin to develop your Innovation Strategy and discuss innovation with other organizational leaders. Next we will take a look at the Innovation PACT, which outlines four principles that leadership must adopt to create sustainable innovation. Before we do that, let's do a quick recap. You should be able to answer the following questions before proceeding to the next section.

- What is the definition of innovation?

- What is the role of an Innovation Strategy?

- What types of environments support innovation, and what changes can you make in your organization to remove innovation roadblocks?

- What is an Ideation System and how can it help your organization be more innovative?

- What are the four types of innovation, and which ones are most important to creating sustainable innovation?

- Who are your audiences and what role does each play in your Innovation Strategy?

The goal of this book is to equip you with the knowledge and resources you need to implement a comprehensive Innovation Strategy and provide a clear path to follow. By understanding the concepts outlined in this section and taking action on the following sections, you are creating an environment where innovation can flourish.

Any organization can improve the level of innovation currently taking place. It just takes a little planning and concentrated effort. Innovation is not difficult. As a matter of fact, it comes quite naturally. Unfortunately, as organizations grow in size, they inadvertently build barriers that make innovation more and more difficult. That does not have to be the case in your organization, and I am going to show your how. It all starts with the next section where you will *take the Innovation PACT*.

Section 2
Take the Innovation PACT

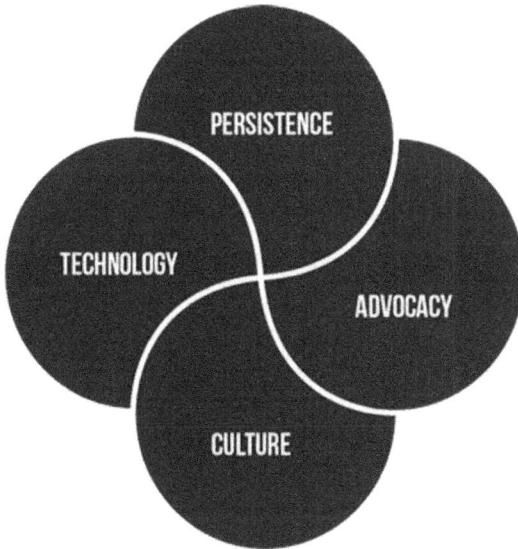

Figure 2a. The PACT in Innovation PACT stands for Persistence, Advocacy, Culture, and Technology. These four components outline the mind-set an organization needs to adopt and promote sustainable innovation.

Now that you have a solid understanding of innovation, it is time to take the Innovation PACT. The Innovation PACT outlines the four components every organization needs to create sustainable innovation: Persistence, Advocacy, Culture, and Technology. Understanding these components is critical to the success of your Innovation Strategy. Let's take a look at each of them in more detail.

Persistence

I hate to be the bearer of bad news, but there is no magic pill or overnight remedy for increasing innovation. It takes time. Depending on where your organization is, this could require a number of changes to your overall culture. The good news is that any organization can become more innovative if it puts in the effort.

Many of the changes required to promote innovation involve an organization's leadership and culture. As you already know, these types of changes can be difficult. As you start to implement your Innovation Strategy and adopt the concepts in the Innovation PACT, you cannot give up. There will undoubtedly be times when it seems like some leadership initiatives are not working, or when one mistake unravels all the progress you have made. But nothing worth doing comes easy, so stay persistent.

If you follow and stick to the steps in this book, your organization will become more innovative. Persistence will overcome any of the challenges you face, and small wins will go a long way. Over time, innovation will snowball and pick up momentum. Then nothing will be able to get in its way.

Advocacy

Over the past few years, there has been a trend of hiring Chief Innovation Officers, where a person who serves as the face of innovation for the organization. This is great, but you do not have to create a full-time position to be successful at innovation. In fact, sometimes hiring a Chief Innovation Officer can hurt your efforts.

Many organizations think that hiring a Chief Innovation Officer will solve all their innovation problems, but that is usually not the case. It takes more than just an individual to make innovation successful. While this does not diminish the value of having a Chief Innovation Officer, it's important to keep an eye out for unrealistic expectations.

I prefer the approach of appointing an Innovation Advocacy team. Innovation Advocacy is an integral part of your overall Innovation Strategy, and the team approach is more sustainable. Depending on available resources, this team can consist of existing employees or you can create new positions. Accordingly, you do not have to add full-time positions if the responsibilities are spread among a few people. The most important thing is to do what works best for your organization.

So what do Innovation Advocates do? They have a number of responsibilities. They are in charge of taking your Innovation Strategy and executing it, but that is not all. Let's take a look at their primary responsibilities in more detail.

Face of the Innovation Strategy

Innovation Advocates will be the innovation mascots for the organization, talking about innovation as much as possible and championing innovative projects. This includes face time at all organization-wide events and hosting events of their own. This will be a constant reminder that innovation is an organizational priority and that there are resources available to support this effort.

If you take a team approach, you should make sure that the members are from a diverse group of functional areas throughout the organization. The members must be savvy in their respectful areas and well liked among their fellow employees. They will also be the face of innovation for your external audience, so they will need to foster those relationships and work with your public relations team.

The person leading the innovation team must also be well respected. He or she should be able to speak well in front of groups, have a broad understanding of the organization, and be included in high-level strategy discussions.

Whether you go with a team or individual approach, the Lead Innovation Advocate should be a part of your top-level leadership team. This shows that you are committed to innovation and allows you to use innovation as a resource when facing challenges that can have a large impact on the organization.

Developing and Maintaining the Strategy

Once you have decided that you are going to move forward with an Innovation Strategy, you will need to identify the

Lead Innovation Advocate. This will be the Innovation Officer, or the person selecting and leading the innovation team. When you start working on the Innovation Strategy, it is important to get this person involved early on. This will ensure that he or she has a full understanding of the entire strategy and that everyone is on the same page.

Innovation Strategy Development

The initial development of the Innovation Strategy will be a combined effort between organizational leadership and the Lead Innovation Advocate. We will cover the components of an Innovation Strategy in Section 3, but for now it is important to understand that this is a group effort. You will need the buy-in of both the Innovation Advocate and leadership to make the strategy successful. Taking this approach will also help ensure that there are no misunderstandings as to the intent of the strategy.

The amount of responsibility you give to the Lead Innovation Advocate during the strategy-development process is your call. If the person is in a full-time position, you should let him or her take charge. If it doesn't involve a full-time position, you should have the person pull together a team first so that he or she has a few more resources to work with. Be sure you have identified who is responsible for what, and then set strict deadlines so that the project does not get delayed or fizzle out.

Innovation Strategy Maintenance

Once you have an Innovation Strategy in place, you must maintain it. It is intended to be a living document, with some sections changing frequently and others being reviewed annually. The Innovation Advocates will lead the charge here.

During the annual review, you may initiate changes to the core sections of the Innovation Strategy, which should be presented to organizational leadership for approval. You may also want to get input from other people inside or outside the organization to support your decision-making process. Innovation Advocates can request input from any number of people, as their reach can be quite high. That is why it is important to involve leadership so that no feathers get ruffled.

Overseeing Innovation Programs

Innovation Programs are a lot of work, and this is where Innovation Advocates will spend a large percentage of their time. This includes moderating the Ideation System, identifying programs, filtering results, and presenting ideas to the selection committee.

Innovation Programs are broken down into six steps that walk you through the entire process. I will provide a detailed overview of each of these steps and more in Section 4.

Staying Updated on Innovation Topics

Innovation is a field that is constantly evolving, with new research being conducted all the time. Therefore, Innovation Advocates must stay up-to-date on what is happening. This will require keeping up with new information, tools, techniques, and even accomplishments by other organizations.

This is important to note, because it means that some financial resources may need to be allocated for education. This could involve formal or informal training, along with membership to innovation sites and/or publications. The innovation team should submit an annual budget that includes expenses related to software, training, meals, memberships, and other educational resources.

The Innovation PACT website will be a great resource for Innovation Advocates to keep up with the latest ideas. I encourage everyone involved in the Innovation Strategy to use it as a resource. The information on the site is tailored directly for organizations that have gone through the process outlined in this book.

Providing Innovation Training

When individuals participate in training, both creativity and productivity increase. Training may not always yield lasting results, but it is important to provide and utilize this as a tool to increase innovation.

The Innovation Advocates will be responsible for providing training to staff, leadership, and possibly the external audience. They can bring in speakers, recruit speakers from within the organization, or present the information themselves. As long as the advocates moderate the training and the speaker is effective, it does not matter who is providing the training.

Facilitate these trainings periodically, but to achieve the maximum benefit, time them with the launch of an Innovation Program. The spike in creativity after a great training session can be the perfect catalyst to spark ideas to solve that next challenge. This will provide you with the highest return for the time your employees spend away at training.

Removing Innovation Roadblocks

There are many roadblocks to innovation: incompetent managers, bad policies, lack of resources, and any number of other things. The goal of Innovation Advocates is to identify and remove these barriers. Again, it is important to have leadership buy in on the Innovation Strategy, as some of the things the Innovation Advocates bring forward may be controversial or even challenge people's jobs. Remember, innovation is change, and change is not always easy. Leadership must stand behind Innovation Advocates and help remove roadblocks.

Gathering Success Stories and Recognizing Innovators

Today's organizations are fast-paced. It can seem like we are on to the next thing before we even have a chance to stop and reflect on what we just accomplished. It is important to recognize the successes you achieve so that you do not forget them. There will be times during your innovation initiatives when things are tough, but having these success stories in your back pocket can motivate your organization to power through the challenges.

When success stories present themselves, it is the responsibility of the Innovation Advocates to capture them. The goal is to constantly celebrate successes and recognize innovators. There are many ways this can be accomplished, whether at a public event or one on one. This could be as simple as a ten-dollar gift card or as elaborate as a comprehensive point system that allows employees to buy prizes, such as days off. While it's true that large organizations provide significant rewards to their employees for great ideas, you can find a way that makes sense for your employees and your budget.

However your organization decides to celebrate, be sure to recognize people when they do something innovative. By sharing these successes with the organization, you will let people know that you value innovation. This will be a constant reminder to employees that you will not accept the status quo.

Culture

Organizational culture is the main differentiator of highly innovative companies, and the reason why some organizations have to acquire or borrow innovation and others seem to never stop generating their own. It is what attracts innovators to your organization and keeps them there. Organizations that build effective innovation cultures will receive the full benefits innovation has to offer.

Sustainable innovation hinges on the culture of the organization. This is the most important element of the Innovation PACT and must be taken seriously. If a culture is built correctly, you will see a significant increase in overall creativity.

Creating a culture of innovation is a leadership undertaking that can demand a significant investment in time and resources, but it is well worth it. To make it easy, I have outlined the four components of an innovative culture. Let's take a look at each one individually.

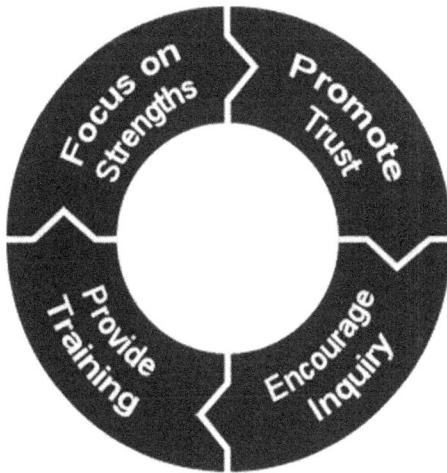

Figure 2b. The four components for promoting a culture of innovation.

Promote Trust

Trust is important because individuals have to feel like they are able to do what they think is right. This includes the ability to make mistakes without having to worry about harsh repercussions. Innovation is an iterative process that often requires tweaks and adjustments to get things right. These tweaks and adjustments are commonly considered failures, which is unfortunate because most organizations do not reward failure. Indeed, most treat it like it is the end of the world.

The goal of leadership should be to allow individuals to fail. This may sound counterproductive, but little failures rarely cause big problems. It is when the organization does not treat failure as part of the learning process that it gets into trouble. In this type of culture, employees tend to hide failures, until those failures grow so big that real damage is done.

Failure is part of the learning process. The faster individuals can fail, learn, and adjust, the faster innovation will happen. If leadership puts too much pressure on perfection, fewer people will try new things; when a failure does happen, it will likely grow into a bigger problem.

So how do you promote trust and allow small failures? You start by constantly communicating to employees that failure within reason is acceptable. You recognize that taking a new journey may have some bumps along the way. Then you acknowledge individuals for making the effort to be innovative, even when they may not have been successful. Do this, and there is a higher likelihood that they will be successful in the future.

Another good way to promote trust is to train managers to delegate more and try to rid the organization of micromanagement. We are in the information age, so the entire idea of knowledge is relative. Ability, adaptability, persistence, and work ethic will trump knowledge any day. A good manager knows this and allows his or her people to develop.

The bottom line is that trust is important in any organization, whether you are trying to be more innovative or not. There are many things you can do to promote trust, but at the end of the day, it is a two-way street. Be generous in trusting others, and others will likely do the same.

Encourage Inquiry

Now more than ever before in history, we have access to staggering amounts of information. This means that we can be knowledgeable on nearly anything with just a little time and effort—all we need to know are the right questions to ask. This is why it is becoming the norm for successful people to be proficient at asking questions, even if they are not necessarily the so-called experts in their field. They are the ones who know what questions to ask to get the information they need. They use the power of inquiry to filter information and arrive at precisely what they are looking for.

Accordingly, inquiry also allows us to define our organizational challenges. The better we are at describing the challenge, the faster we can move toward a solution. This can seem difficult at first, but once you get the hang of it, it is quite easy.

So how can you encourage this type of appreciative inquiry? It starts with teaching leadership, team leads, and managers to ask good questions. By modeling this behavior, they can embolden others to ask questions in their day-to-day interactions: open-ended questions and questions that get to the very root of the challenge. This will ensure a complete understanding of the situation.

Another ways to promote inquiry is through training and constant reinforcement. Hearing the words, "That is a great question," makes everyone feel good. Read Warren Berger's book, *A More Beautiful Question*, for more tips and information. He explains how you can spark breakthrough ideas with the use of inquiry. It is an ambitious goal, but every leader should strive for it.

Provide Training

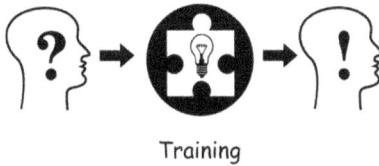

Training

Figure 2c: Training is often the missing puzzle piece between a current problem and the idea for the solution.

Training is often overlooked—therefore, I will say this a thousand times if I have to: training is often the missing puzzle piece between having a problem and knowing a solution. Organizations need to make sure that they have a systematic approach in place concerning how employees are trained and developed. Every employee should have some sort of training and development plan that outlines both the person's strengths and development areas so that you can easily track progress. Additionally, allowing employees to work in other areas or on special projects provides them with opportunities to try new things that they find interesting, which can lead to greater employee growth and satisfaction.

This approach has an added benefit: not only does it contribute to the employee's overall knowledge and ability to perform his or her job duties, but it can also have a great impact on the organization itself. Having a fresh perspective on a new topic can lead to innovative ideas that have been overlooked by individuals who spend a lot of time working in that area.

Training is often the first thing that is cut when budgets are tight. If you want to stay innovative, you will want to reconsider this move. Cutting training is not the best option.

Focus on Strengths

Find someone who truly loves his or her job, and I can practically guarantee that person is good at that job. If the person is not good now, he or she will be soon. This is because that job most likely plays to the person's strengths. If you focus on employee strengths, passion and motivation are easy to spark. This leads to overall fulfillment and, more important for the organization, results.

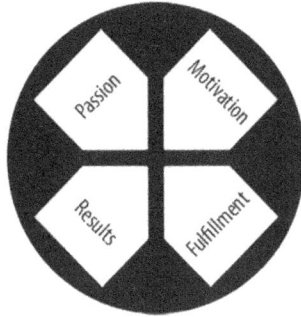

Figure 2d. By focusing on an individual's strengths, you can use that person's passion to produce exceptional results.

We all have strengths, and doing something we are good at feels rewarding. Although it is not always possible to utilize an employee's strengths in his or her daily job, innovative projects can be an excellent opportunity to showcase them. That is why leadership must identify the strengths of its people and find ways to bring those strengths out.

Leadership can harness the power of passion by closely aligning people with their individual strengths as much as possible. Sometimes this requires working with other departments or placing employees on special projects that take them away from their day-to-day work—but believe me, it's worth it. Happier employees will be more productive and more creative in all areas of their job.

The investment you make by allowing individuals to develop their strengths will produce notable returns in your innovation initiatives. Allowing people to have different strengths provides different perspectives. This will lead to noteworthy dialogue and produce creative solutions to organizational problems.

Technology

Technology is not just a tool to achieve innovation; it is also the catalyst for innovation. We are in the information age, and the impact of technology is still in its infancy. Technology is becoming the lifeblood of organizations, and the ones that do not use it correctly quickly find themselves on life support.

Leaders must take the necessary steps to make sure technology gets the respect it deserves. Many of your new programs or initiatives will have a technology component.

But many leaders continue to treat technology as a utility instead of a partner.

Technology can help reshape entire business areas. Therefore, you must include it at the strategic level. If you don't, you could be spending a lot of time, money, and effort retrofitting technology into an inefficient process.

In my experience, I have come across three different types of leaders:

- Leaders who treat technology as a last resort

- Leaders who support technology for the sake of technology

- Leaders who are educated on technology and support it for the right reasons

It does not take much thought to figure out which type of leader is the best. Leaders who are educated on technology and support it for the right reasons will get the best results. They will also be less likely to fall victim to technology bloat or inefficient processes.

This is so important because technology acumen is not typically a quality that organizations look for in top-level leadership. Don't be fooled. If you are a leader, understanding technology is just as important as understanding money. You do not need to get a master's degree in technology or computer science, but you must make an effort to keep up with the latest trends and how they impact your organization and field.

This is not to discredit technology professionals. They are very smart, but great ones can be difficult to find, and it can be challenging for them to understand your overall strategy and how technology relates to organizational goals. As a leader, it will be your job to relate them and let the technology professional figure out the technical aspects. By asking good questions, you can put the puzzle pieces together to build innovative solutions.

Wrap-Up

In this section we discussed the four components of the Innovation PACT, which are the steps that will help change your organizational culture into one where innovation can flourish. Next we are going to look at the components that make up the Innovation Strategy.

The Innovation PACT will be included in your Innovation Strategy, but it is something that will have to be worked on independently. Leadership must buy in to these four components if you want to create sustainable innovation. Some will come naturally and some will take work, but all are necessary.

Let's take a look at them one more time before we move forward.

Persistence	Be **persistent** in your innovation efforts. Highly innovative organizations do not give up on innovation. It is not always easy but if you stick with it, you will see results.
Advocacy	Innovation **Advocates** are the heart of your Innovation Strategy. Finding good people and providing them with adequate resources will help spread your innovation efforts to every sector of your organization.
Culture	Leadership must create a **culture** in which innovation can flourish. Leadership sets the tone for the organization, and innovative organizations set a tone of innovation.
Technology	**Technology** is constantly providing new opportunities for organizations to be more innovative. Understanding and embracing technology for the right reasons is a key component in your innovation efforts.

Commit to the components outlined in this Innovation PACT and you will see benefits. You can download the Innovation PACT graphic for free under the resources section at http://www.InnovationPACT.com. Print it and display it in as many places as possible, as it clearly outlines your core values for innovation. By adopting these principles, you will begin to see the significance of creating an organization that welcomes innovation instead of one that impedes it.

Let's move on to Section 3, where we will take a look at what needs to be included in your Innovation Strategy.

Section 3

Innovation Strategy Components

Now it is time to take what we have learned so far and focus on how to build your Innovation Strategy. This is where the book becomes more of a reference guide or handbook. I encourage you to read through this section once, and then refer to it frequently as you develop your Innovation Strategy.

When you are starting out, it is important to understand all of the components in the Innovation Strategy. However, I do not expect you to come out of this section having memorized each one. To provide a clear picture of what your Innovation Strategy looks like, I have created the Innovation Strategy Framework. Let's take a brief look at that before we jump into the Innovation Strategy components.

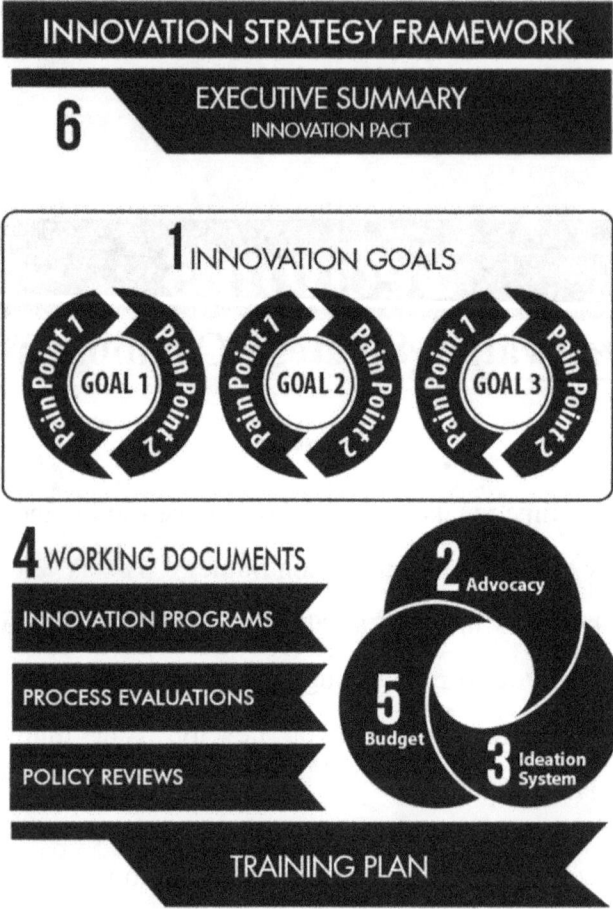

Figure 3a. The Innovation Strategy Framework outlines all of the components of the Innovation Strategy. The numbers specify the order in the process that each item should be completed.

Innovation Strategy Framework Overview

The Innovation Strategy Framework is a graphical representation of the Innovation Strategy. You will notice that there are numbers next to each section in the graphic; these represent the order in which each section should be created. Please note that we will be covering these sections in the order that they will appear in your completed Innovation Strategy and not in the order that they should be created. This may be a little confusing now, but if you use the step-by-step guide provided later in this book, it will walk you through everything.

Below is a brief description of each section in the Innovation Strategy Framework. We will go through these in more detail, but this high-level overview will provide you with a better understanding of how everything fits together.

Innovation Strategy Framework Components

- **Introduction:** The introduction includes the cover page, table of contents, modification history, and Executive Summary. Ironically, this is the last thing that you will develop because it is hard to introduce something before you know exactly what it is.

- **Innovation PACT:** The Innovation PACT section is a reminder of the importance of persistence, advocacy, culture, and technology in your Innovation Strategy. This section should include the Innovation PACT graphic and may include additional information on how you will accomplish it.

- **Goals:** The goals section includes your high-level Innovation Goals and Organizational Pain Points. It sets the focus for your Innovation Strategy and makes sure your innovation initiatives align with your overall strategy.

- **Advocacy:** The advocacy section will outline your approach to innovation advocacy and set the roles and responsibilities of the Innovation Advocates.

- **Ideation System:** The Ideation System section will cover your formal innovation process. It will outline how ideas are submitted, selected, and implemented.

- **Innovation Budget:** The innovation budget section will cover how your Innovation Strategy is funded. It will not include the actual costs, but will outline how funds are allocated to make sure that the Innovation Strategy receives funding in the future.

- **Working Documents:** The Working Documents section will include numerous documents the Innovation Advocates will use to keep the Innovation Strategy moving forward. This will include your Training Plan, Policy Review List, Process Evaluation List, and Innovation Programs.

The rest of this section will cover each of the Innovation Strategy components in more detail. The framework provides a simplified approach for you to work on these individually and plug them into the Innovation Strategy. The goal is to be as efficient and effective as possible when creating the Innovation Strategy. This framework, along with the resources provided, should accomplish that goal.

Resources

A number of resources are available to help get you started on all of the components in this section. Additional information on these is provided throughout this section, denoted by resource boxes. You can also find all of the resources at http://www.InnovationPACT.com. These are only a starting point, so feel free to add additional components. Just make sure to cover everything included in this section.

Now let's take a look at each of the core Innovation Strategy Components.

Executive Summary

As with most formal documents, it is a good idea to have some type of summary. This will provide readers with a short synopsis so that they can get a quick understanding of what is included.

The Innovation Strategy should be short enough so that anyone can skim through it, but it is best to play it safe and include an Executive Summary. It should be developed by top-level leadership and outline why innovation is important for the organization. It should serve as an introduction to the strategy, show the reader how it should be used, and include the living documents that will live outside of the strategy. It will provide good insight into how innovation is being implemented in the organization.

What to Include in Your Executive Summary

Below are a few ideas that you should consider including in your Executive Summary:

- Top two to three Innovation Goals

- Top two to three Pain Points for each goal

- Ideation System overview

- Funding resources

- Innovation PACT overview

- Key leadership involved

We will not put too many guidelines around the Executive Summary because it really should be something that is unique to each organization. Having one in place is the important part. As you complete the other components of the Innovation Strategy, the Executive Summary will start to become clear. It is a good idea to complete all other Innovation Strategy components prior to starting this.

Once it is completed, you will want to update the Executive Summary when you update the strategy. Updating the entire Innovation Strategy should be part of the budgeting process. It is a good idea to do it around budget time so that any additional funds that will be required can be accounted for. This should take place at least once a year, but you can review it more frequently than that if you think it will be beneficial.

Drafting the Executive Summary

Once you have completed the rest of the Innovation Strategy components, the Executive Summary should all but write itself. Take a look at the Innovation Goals, Organizational Pain Points, advocacy, and living documents to get started. This will give you a good idea of what it is you are trying to accomplish by implementing an Innovation Strategy.

You will also want to keep the word count limited in this section. Sometimes it is better to focus on graphics or lists if possible. It may take a little time to get it right, but remember that this may be the only part of the strategy some people read. Therefore, it is important to make it easy to understand.

Lastly, get as many people to review it as you can, and make sure some of those people are not overly familiar with the Innovation Strategy initiative. This will give you an unbiased opinion. If your reviewers have comments, be sure to take them into consideration. Being familiar with the Innovation Strategy can put up blinders that can result in missing information. This gives you the opportunity to be sure the message is clear and concise to all who read it.

Approaching the Executive Summary in this manner ensures that you craft a document that is both easy to understand and effective.

Resource: Innovation Strategy Template

The Innovation Strategy Template will provide some additional guidance on creating this section, but it is really left to your creativity. Start with some of the ideas presented in the template and build on that. Be creative and have fun with it!

Innovation PACT

Every organization should start with taking the Innovation PACT. Without succeeding in those areas, there is little chance that your organization will be successful at becoming more innovative. Innovation requires an environment in which it can flourish, and the PACT enables that. That is why it comes before everything else in terms of your timeline, even though there is little work required on your part.

Including the Innovation PACT in your strategy is easy. The graphic can simply be inserted as is. You do not have to modify it or list any specific initiatives; it is only there to serve as a reminder to the readers of the importance of each component.

Resource: Innovation Strategy Template

The Innovation Strategy Template will include the Innovation PACT as the first section. Feel free to add additional initiatives or information if you have any. If not, just include the graphic.

> **Resource: Innovation PACT Graphic**
>
> If you are using the Innovation Strategy Template, it will already be included. If you are starting from scratch or just want the graphic for other uses, it is available as a separate resource. Feel free to use it however and as frequently as you would like.

Innovation Goals

Organizations have different reasons for looking at innovation. What are yours? That is the question you should answer in the Innovation Goals section. Are you implementing innovation to save money or increase morale? Are you doing it to compete in the marketplace or operate at your highest potential? Whatever your reasons are, they should be documented. Determining what is behind your motivation for implementing an Innovation Strategy provides a clear picture of where the focus will be.

This will be the first step in creating a consistent Innovation Strategy. The next component we will look at is identifying Organizational Pain Points. This might seem a little redundant, but I assure you that this is not the case. If you take a look at the goals section in the Innovation Strategy Framework, you will see how the pain points and Innovation Goals fit together.

Figure 3b. Start by developing your Innovation Goals and then identify one to two objectives or pain points for each goal.

To simplify things, you can treat goals as high-level categories and pain points as more detailed objectives in each of the categories. Goals will rarely change throughout iterations to the Innovation Strategy, but Organizational Pain Points will be frequently added and removed. By starting with goals, we help make sure the overall strategy is in alignment with the big picture.

Developing Your Innovation Goals

The goal—pun intended—is to identify three to five high-level goals for your Innovation Strategy. Selecting goals will require a bit of work because you want to make sure you have everyone on board.

The best place to start is to look at your organization's mission and core values. Can innovation help meet those targets? If so, this should be noted. Let's take a look at an approach you can use to help develop your Innovation Goals:

1. Pull together key people from the organization and have them write down a few of their top goals. If it makes sense, you may also want to include your external audience, because they may have a different perspective. Once you have the group identified, ask them to think "big picture" and focus on goals that would provide the most overall benefit to the organization.

2. Filter out any goals that are overly specific or do not address problems that have a large impact on the organization.

3. Review the goals and combine any that are similar or overlap. Make sure each goal is clearly stated in a single paragraph.

4. Have as many people as you can get involved with ranking the goals. You have the option of including a wider audience, or you can keep it at the top leadership level.

5. Identify the top three to five goals. Aim for three goals, but if four and five are ranked close to the top three, you can incorporate them as well. Include goals in your Innovation Strategy.

Each goal should be listed in a title and statement form. Make sure the goals are action based by stating exactly what it is you would like to accomplish. The clearer the goal, the easier it will be to identify Organizational Pain Points.

When we move to Organizational Pain Points, we will try to identify reasons why we are not meeting the goal currently.

These pain points will be used by the Innovation Advocates to create Innovation Programs. That is why it is important to make sure that the goals you have identified are important to the organization.

Resource: Innovation Strategy Template

The Innovation Strategy Template will provide some additional guidance on creating your organizational goals. It will also include some example goals.

Start by reviewing them and then go through the process outlined in this section. It may take a little time, but it will be worth the effort once you see the results from your Innovation Programs.

Organizational Pain Points

Identifying Organizational Pain Points is a critical step that will help direct your efforts. You may have already done something similar in other strategic planning exercises, but this should be done separately and should be specifically focused with an eye toward innovation. Take a look at your high-level goals and identify pain points or roadblocks standing in the way of achieving them.

Let's start by taking a look at some common Organizational Pain Points:

- Trouble attracting and retaining talent

- Low customer-service ratings

- Slow product-development life cycle

- Large number of project failures

- Decreased sales or increased competition

These are some basic examples. Every organization has something it would like to be better at. The goal is to try to identify what those things are. Then you can use your Innovation Programs and other innovation initiatives to help get there.

Identifying Your Organizational Pain Points

There are numerous tools out there to help identify Organizational Pain Points. Some organizations may want to do a formal assessment, such as a SWOT or PEST analysis. This is especially beneficial at the onset, but it can be very time-consuming and costly. Other organizations may choose to pull in a few leaders from around the organization and do some brainstorming over lunch or in an afternoon meeting. This works too as long as you have a good group of leaders who understand the organization.

Do not let your Innovation Strategy stall during the pain-point-identification process. Find something that has a good balance between accuracy and effort. It does not have to be perfect; since you will be reviewing this annually at a minimum, you will have an opportunity to change it down the road.

This process will be very similar to goal identification with a few minor changes. You already have the goals identified, so you will be focusing directly on each of these. Start with one to two pain points under each goal in the beginning. Most organizations will not be able to work on more than a handful of pain points in a single year, so having a small number of options to choose from is not necessarily a bad thing.

Once you have identified your pain points, you will need to describe them as well as possible in short paragraphs. After you have detailed them, you will need to also explain the intended results (if known) in the same format. By providing the pain point and the desired results, you give enough information to the Innovation Advocates to implement a focused Innovation Program.

Resource: Innovation Strategy Template

The Innovation Strategy Template will provide some additional guidance on identifying your Organizational Pain Points. You can also review the examples in this section.

Take one goal at a time, and go through the pain-point-selection process for each. Narrow the pain points down to the top one or two for each goal. Then list the title, pain point, desired outcome, and overarching goal for each.

Advocacy

We discussed advocacy in great detail in Section 2. Now we will take a look at how to formalize it. Start by deciding how many people will be involved in advocacy. Are you going to have a team or a single individual? Once you have decided that, you can begin to define their roles and responsibilities. This will include the selection process, membership terms, position in the company, and primary duties.

I always recommend having a team of individuals to handle Innovation Advocacy. This does not have to be their full-time job, but they do need to have some time to dedicate to it. They also need to be tech savvy, well liked, good communicators, and team players; they should have a good understanding of their respective areas and how they fit into the overall organization.

If you prefer the individual approach, make sure they have the same skills but a much broader understanding of the organization. The individual approach does provide some sustainability challenges, but it is preferred by some organizations. I believe in all situations you should have a team, even if the team is only acting in an advisory role to the Lead Innovation Advocate.

You will need to work with the Innovation Advocates to define their roles and responsibilities. The primary responsibilities are listed here for your convenience; however, Section 2 covers each of these in greater detail:

- Be the face of the Innovation Strategy.

- Develop and maintain the Innovation Strategy.

- Oversee Innovation Programs.

- Stay updated on innovation topics.

- Provide innovation training.

- Remove innovation roadblocks.

- Gather success stories and recognize innovators.

In addition to these, you will most likely need to add other responsibilities, such as providing regular updates to leadership, producing an innovation newsletter, hosting an innovation awards ceremony, and so forth. Be creative, but do not overdo it.

To make it easy to update the Innovation Advocates' responsibilities, you should create a separate document instead of adding them directly into the Innovation Strategy. If you take the individual approach, include the responsibilities in the job description. That way you can tie those responsibilities directly to the person's job functions.

Either way, you want to provide clear expectations for your Innovation Advocates.

Lastly, you want to make sure to clearly identify where the person or team fits in the organization. You should include the Lead Innovation Advocate in top-level leadership meetings. This is especially important early on, as there will be a lot of information that surfaces, and you want to take action as quickly as possible. If you are not able to include the Innovation Advocate in leadership meetings, you should at least schedule regular meetings for status updates. This should be thoughtfully considered to ensure that your organizational structure itself does not quash innovation efforts.

Formalizing Your Innovation Advocacy Efforts

If you are taking the team approach, completing this section will take some time. You should identify the first Lead Innovation Advocate and allow that person to pull together a team. If you are taking the individual approach, you need to create a job description and hire someone. As previously suggested, I believe that creating a team is the best way to achieve optimal results.

To create your innovation team, you should have your Lead Innovation Advocate handpick the first group. If you have identified a strong leader for this position, he or she will be able to pull together a diverse but highly functional group of people. If your leader is having trouble with this, you can also provide some guidance.

Next, have the team meet and develop its roles and responsibilities. You can provide team members with the template and an introduction, but try to get them involved early on. If it is not perfect, you can provide comments before approving it. Once the selection is finalized, have the advocates schedule regular meetings so that they can begin to work through the Innovation Strategy.

Remember to leave the responsibilities in a separate document. This is important because it allows you to modify them directly without having to touch the Innovation Strategy. It will take some time, but do not get caught up in making it perfect in the beginning. It can be developed over time and modified as needed. Just capture as much of the responsibilities as you can so that the Innovation Advocates are aware of exactly what is expected of them.

Resource: Innovation Strategy Template

The Innovation Strategy Template is designed for the team approach, but you can modify it as needed. The template will include some basic language and reference the complete roles and responsibilities as a separate document.

Use these resources as a starting point. You can modify them in any way you wish, and I suggest personalizing them with your letterhead, logo, standard language, and so forth. The resources cover all of the important responsibilities you should include and provide some additional language to make sure you have the necessary controls in place.

> **Resource: Innovation Team Roles and Responsibilities**
>
> The Roles and Responsibilities Template provides some of the basic responsibilities. Use the document as a starting point and then add any additional information as needed. If there are additional responsibilities, add them once you have completed the basic information.
>
> **Resource: Innovation Officer Job Description**
>
> If you choose the individual approach, you can use the Innovation Officer Job Description as a starting point. You can take the core responsibilities and add them to your job description template. Then add additional responsibilities that are required by the position.

Ideation System

The Ideation System will outline your process for taking an idea from conception all the way through implementation. It can be anything from a locked box in a break room to the implementation of sophisticated software. The primary purpose of the Ideation System is to support your formal Innovation Programs. Your Innovation Programs will allow you to address specific Organizational Pain Points that need to be resolved to turn the programs into action. That is where the Ideation System comes in.

Figure 3c. The Ideation System outlines the process an idea goes through, from problem identification through implementation.

Let's take a look at the components included in most Ideation Systems:

1. **Submittal:** This is where ideas are submitted. This can be through formal Ideation software or through a manual process such as e-mail or even paper. That's right, even the time-honored suggestion box can be an innovation tool. However, if you are the skeptical type, avoid any system that has the possibility of hanging chads.

2. **Ranking:** Once ideas are submitted, they need to be ranked. Ranking can be handled inside the Ideation software or done by a selected group of individuals. The ideas that are ranked the highest move on to selection.

3. **Selection:** Idea selection should have leadership involvement. Ideas are selected based on their ranking, applicability, feasibility, and other factors important to the organization. During this process, ideas may also need to be refined so that they can be implemented.

4. **Implementation:** Typically you would only be implementing one or two ideas. The team or leader in charge of implementing the ideas should be a subject-matter expert in that specific area. This may not be the person that submitted the idea, but you will want to provide feedback to that person and keep the Innovation Advocates involved.

5. **Reward:** You should reward people for participating in the Innovation Program, especially those who have ideas that were ranked high or selected for

implementation. This is also a great opportunity for the Innovation Advocates to gather lessons learned and success stories.

The Innovation PACT plays a big role in your Ideation System. As you can see from the graphic, you need leadership and an innovative culture to make these things happen. You will also need to define each component of the Ideation System in your Innovation Strategy. The Innovation Advocates will spend a lot of time conducting Innovation Programs, and the Ideation System is the backbone.

That being said, do not get too caught up in the process of selecting software or a manual process. Define your system first, and then find the solution that fits the system the best. There are many benefits to taking the software approach, but sometimes implementation can get very complex. Therefore, do what you are comfortable with and be sure that whatever route you choose, you have the appropriate resources to manage it.

Defining Your Ideation System

You have a good deal of flexibility when defining your Ideation System. I will provide some input here, but every organization should handle this in a way that makes sense for them. However, I do not want to leave you in the dark, so here are some steps that can help you along the way:

1. First, decide how you want ideas to be ranked and selected. If you want this to be handled by a small team, then a lower-tech solution can work. If you want ideas to be ranked by your entire organization, then you will need a software tool. There are not many differences in the actual process after you have made this decision. Just be sure to note your selection, because you will need to further define it in the ranking and selection sections.

2. Once you have decided how ideas will be ranked and selected, it is time to identify who is in charge. Define who will be in charge of ranking ideas and who will be in charge of selecting an idea. This may be a multiple-step process, so be sure to include all of the steps.

3. Next, it's time to define how ideas will be submitted. If this will be a formal process, you will probably use some sort of software. Now is a good time to start looking at software options to find a solution that works for you. If you will be using a manual process, you can simply outline the details here.

4. Now let's move on to implementation. There may not be much information in the Innovation Strategy on implementation because this will fall back on the business units. However, make sure that an Innovation Advocate is involved throughout the implementation process and that there is a way to handle funding issues. You can leave this section flexible because it may be difficult to anticipate every scenario.

5. Specify the reward system. You may already have a reward system in place, and I am not suggesting that you create a new one just for innovation. Just make sure you are rewarding innovation, and put something in the Innovation Strategy so people know

it. You can also pull some of this out into a separate document if you think it will change frequently.

There are a few more considerations if you are implementing formal Ideation software. For instance, you may need to identify the software administrators, usage policies, and accessibility. If you are using a manual system, you may still have some of the same considerations. Be sure to consider all aspects from start to finish for this process, and define each step the best that you can.

Resource: Innovation Strategy Template

Defining and implementing an Ideation System can be a little overwhelming, but the resources provided in the Innovation Strategy Template significantly simplify this process. The template walks you through step by step.

Innovation Budget

You can implement an Innovation Strategy for a relatively low cost. However, you do want to make sure you have allocated the necessary funds to keep things moving forward. Organizations will find these funds in different ways. Make sure you identify how these funds will be secured so that they continue to be available in future years. This is critical to the longevity of your Innovation Strategy.

Most of the expenses will be dedicated to the Innovation Advocates so that they can access the resources required to perform their duties. Here are some of the common expenses typically found in an innovation budget:

- **Ideation Software:** If you go with Ideation software, you will most likely have some type of ongoing software and maintenance fees in addition to the up-front costs of the initial purchase.

- **Training:** It is important that Innovation Advocates have access to training so that they can keep up with what is going on in innovation.

- **Membership/Dues:** The innovation team may need to join associations or subscribe to websites or magazines that provide updated information on innovation.

- **Meals:** Lunches for meetings or trainings may be required. Snacks are always good to have around when trying to get people to attend organization-wide trainings.

- **Travel:** Traveling to trainings can be expensive. The Innovation Advocates may also want to travel to other organizations to see examples of innovative projects or technology.

- **Rewards:** This does not necessarily need to be in the innovation budget. Just make sure that whatever innovation rewards you have in place are funded somewhere.

- **Marketing:** If you are planning on facilitating Innovation Programs outside of your organization, you may need to allocate marketing funds. Often in this situation, marketing is required to get the word out about the Innovation Programs. This would include any postage required for mail campaigns.

- **Design/Multimedia:** Most organizations do not have internal design and multimedia resources.

Therefore, you may need to allocate funds to hire experts to develop promotional material.

- **Website/Branding:** This can be included in your design-and-multimedia budget, but I want to touch on it specifically. Some organizations may want to do branding around their Innovation Strategy, which can include logo design, promotional material, and even a website.

- **Office Supplies:** The Innovation Advocates will need access to the necessary supplies to run meetings and conduct brainstorming sessions.

- **Printing:** If you do not have the resources internally, include some funds for professional printing.

It is important to have Innovation Advocates prepare a budget just like any other program or division. The list above is pretty extensive, but it does not have to be expensive. Many of these things may already be available in house, and sharing resources is a good step toward being more innovative. Just make sure that the Innovation Advocates have the resources necessary to keep the strategy moving forward.

Developing Your Innovation Budget

Make sure that the Innovation Strategy covers how the innovation budget is handled and where the funds come from. Don't include the actual numbers in the Innovation Strategy; just outline the process. It should also specify who has authority to spend the money and how purchases are approved and documented.

As for creating the budget, use what you already have in place. If you cannot afford to fund these things up front, don't let it stop you from moving forward. If you've selected the right group, I am positive your Innovation Advocates can come up with some creative ways to make things happen.

Resource: Innovation Strategy Template

The Innovation Strategy Template includes some ideas on how to fund your Innovation Strategy. Figure out what works for your organization and document it in this section.

Do not include any numbers; just focus on how the budget will be prepared, where the funds will come from, and who has authority to approve purchases.

Innovation Strategy Working Documents

Everything we have covered so far makes up the core components of the Innovation Strategy. These will not change very often but should be reviewed annually at a minimum. The items I am going to cover now are the Working Documents for the Innovation Advocates, which will live outside the Innovation Strategy and be updated more frequently. These documents should be reviewed quarterly at a minimum, and components of them will be updated at every innovation-team meeting. Keeping these Working Documents updated will provide a clear picture of what the Innovation Advocates are currently working on.

The Working Documents include three lists—the Innovation Programs List, the Policy Review List, and the Process Evaluation List—and a Training Plan. These simple lists will help keep innovation moving forward in your organization. The Training Plan will outline all innovation training and who the target audience is. This is important for budgeting and to make sure the necessary training is being provided.

Every organization should have these Working Documents in place. It may sound like a lot, but it is important to document your progress and initiatives as a mechanism for measuring results. The Innovation Advocates will be reviewing these documents regularly, and this allows you to keep a pulse on everything in the works. So let's take a look at each of the documents in more detail.

Innovation Programs List

The Innovation Program List is your project list for all of your completed, active, and future Innovation Programs. One of the main responsibilities of the Innovation Advocates is to maintain this list and stay on top of Innovation Programs. This includes identifying new programs and prioritizing them. The Innovation Advocates will review the list at every innovation-team meeting and make any necessary updates.

As Innovation Programs are completed, new programs will need to be added. The Innovation Advocates will review

Organizational Pain Points and try to identify new programs to address them. Once a new program is identified, it should be approved by leadership before being added. This can be done as part of the quarterly meeting with leadership and will help ensure that everyone is on board with the new programs.

There are a few things you will want to track in each Innovation Program. You can customize this list to fit your needs, but the list below contains some of the most common information that is tracked:

- Challenge question (see Section 4)

- Target audience

- Start date

- Completion date

- Outcome

This simple tool will help keep track of all the Innovation Programs and their statuses throughout the year. It will serve as your scorecard and should not be overlooked. Innovation

Advocates should update it monthly at a minimum and provide leadership with a quarterly update. When providing the leadership update, make sure to include any changes and highlight completed programs.

Typically, this document will be a spreadsheet. You do not need to overthink it, however. Do what is simple and what you are familiar with. This advice goes for all of the lists. You can use a spreadsheet, whiteboard, or any one of the numerous software-based project-tracking tools. Just make sure it is easy for any of the Innovation Advocates to review and update.

Resource: Innovation Programs List Template

The Innovation Programs List Template is a simple document that you can use to track your Innovation Programs. There is nothing special about the document, but it may save you a few minutes from having to create it yourself.

Keep all Innovation Programs on the list for the current year, and archive the completed programs annually. It is important to capture your successes in addition to monitoring active and future programs.

Policy Review List

Organizational policies can be one of the biggest roadblocks to innovation. Therefore, it is important that the Innovation Advocates review policies regularly and make recommendations. This is where the Policy Review List comes in. It contains policies that have been identified by leadership or the Innovation Advocates as potential roadblocks.

This list will show completed, active, and future policies that need to be reviewed. Every time a new policy is introduced to the organization, the Innovation Advocates should review it for any potential roadblocks. You will also have to review policies that are already in place. Make it a goal to review all of the policies over time, but start with the ones that can make the biggest impact.

Identifying what policies need to be reviewed is not as straightforward as it may seem. To be proactive, it is important to identify a few policies every year. You cannot expect someone to let you know what policies are preventing innovation—you will have to go out and find them.

Start with obvious policies that tend to have common innovation-blocking rules, such as acceptable use and conduct policies. Oftentimes these well-meaning guidelines inhibit creativity because they are unnecessarily constraining. By reviewing these common offenders, you can demonstrate to your organization that innovation starts at the core.

The actual process of reviewing the policies can be delegated to members of the Innovation Advocacy team. This will allow you to get through more policies in a shorter time frame.

Here is some of the information that should be tracked in your Policy Review List:

- Policy name

- Date last modified

- Target review date

- Suggested changes

- Actual changes

Updating organizational policies will be a collaborative effort; it will most likely require that you work with your HR department and leadership. In an ideal situation, HR will run all new policies through the Innovation Advocacy group. That way, the group will be able to provide comments before the policy becomes active. By working closely with HR and leadership, you can create an environment with as few roadblocks as possible.

Resource: Policy Review List Template

The Policy Review List Template is a simple document to help track your completed, active, and future policies to be reviewed. You will want to keep track of policies so you do not review them again unless changes have been made.

Process Evaluation List

Organizations are made up of processes, and the ability to improve those processes is vital to your overall innovation efforts. I have seen it time and time again where making small changes to a process can have a significant impact on productivity. That is why it is so important to include process evaluations as part of your overall Innovation Strategy.

The Process Evaluation List will serve as a tool to keep track of completed, active, and future processes that need to be evaluated. Innovation Advocates should identify processes to be included on this list. Processes that span across multiple functional areas usually have the most room for improvement because communication barriers create inefficiencies. This is why having a diverse team is important, as team members can identify processes that need improvement in their respective business units.

The evaluation of processes will be delegated to one or two Innovation Advocates, but it is good to keep the entire team updated. Since processes will require that you work with multiple stakeholders, it is important to keep everyone informed as much as possible. The Process Evaluation List will help with that, and it should include the following information on each process:

- Process name

- Business unit(s) involved

- Advocate(s) evaluating the process

- Recommended changes

- Actual changes

- Estimated time and cost savings

- All stakeholders involved

Although you may not have process-evaluation experts on hand, do the best you can with the resources you do have. It does not take an expert to identify glaring inefficiencies.

Start by assigning the process review to one or two Innovation Advocates. Have them shadow the process and bring back their findings. Work closely with the business units because they will often be able to identify inefficiencies right away. Many people know things that can be improved, but just do not feel empowered to make the necessary changes.

After you have completed your evaluation and discussed the results with the Innovation Advocacy Team, take the recommendations to leadership. Work with them and the business units directly to create a solution. This will help ensure that the business unit is on board and that they get credit for making the change.

Once the changes have been made, be sure to showcase the impacts to the rest of the organization. This will help jump-start the momentum of self-evaluating processes.

When business units start improving their own processes, you will see the snowball effect that innovation can have.

Resource: Process Evaluation List Template

The Process Evaluation List is a tool to track completed, active, and future processes to be evaluated. You will want to track these annually and archive completed process evaluations at the end of the year.

Innovation Training Plan

The Innovation Training Plan will consist of two components:

- Section 1: Training for Innovation Advocates

- Section 2: Training for the organization and external audience

It is highly unlikely that any of the Innovation Advocates will be innovation experts on day one, but creating an Innovation Training Plan is the first step to getting them there. It is also important that you are training your organization so that you have collective momentum.

Start with your Innovation Advocates. Training should include individual and group trainings and might consist of books, webinars, conferences, or any other type of training. Once the training has been identified, be sure to list it on the Training Plan. Then you can start training the organization and external audience. Put the Innovation Advocates in charge of running this training, which could incorporate articles, in-person training, guest speakers, or on-demand training.

Organizational training can be further broken down into groups. You may provide additional training for leadership or specific business units. Do what makes sense for your organization. Just make sure to capture all of your training in the Training Plan.

It is not always going to be easy to find training for your organization. Innovation Advocates must make an effort to put on their own training program if they are not able to find any. Providing training is very important, so someone will have to take responsibility for it. This includes training on how to use the Ideation software and an overview of the Innovation Strategy. It is also a good idea to send out some type of regular communication with innovation tips, which will constantly challenge the organization to be on the lookout for opportunities.

It can be very time-consuming to identify training in advance. However, do not let that stop you from moving forward. The Training Plan can be developed over time, and as trainings become available, you can simply add them. If your Innovation Advocates are constantly on the lookout, opportunities will present themselves. This is also why it is so important to make sure that some training funds are available. That way, when training does become available, the Innovation Advocates can take advantage of it.

After a couple of years, you will have a good, solid understanding of your organization's training needs. By using your Training Plan as a resource, you can look back at the previous years to get ideas on future training.

Resource: Innovation Training Plan Template

The Innovation Training Plan Template is a great starting point and includes some ideas to help develop your Training Plan.

It is important to start with the Leading Innovation Presentation (below) for leadership and then focus on the Ideation System and the Ideation software. Once the Innovation Advocates get rolling, they can identify additional training for both themselves and the organization.

Meeting Agenda

The Meeting Agenda is not really a working document, but it is important. Having a good Meeting Agenda in place helps keep all meetings productive, including innovation meetings. It still amazes me how many organizations do not correctly utilize this simple but powerful tool. Please do not be one of them.

Let's take a look at what you should include in your Innovation Advocacy Meeting Agenda:

- **Attendance:** Keep attendance at every meeting. Although I do not believe in rules for rules' sake, there should be an attendance requirement. Your meetings and progress should not be stifled due to a lack of attendance.

- **Scribe:** Have someone take notes at every meeting. This will prevent lost information and stop you from discussing the same thing over and over. Notes should be typed and e-mailed out directly after the meeting.

- **Timekeeper:** There are two rules everyone should have for meetings: start on time and end early. Have someone keep track of the time and end the meeting on or before the set end time.

- **Innovation Programs:** Review the list of Innovation Programs and the status of active programs. As programs move to completion, shuffle things around and add new programs as needed.

- **Policy Reviews:** Review the list of policies that need to be evaluated. This includes an update on any policies that are currently undergoing revision. If changes are recommended, be sure to take action and pass the changes on to the appropriate individuals.

- **Process Evaluations:** Review the list of processes currently being evaluated, discuss any findings, and take action on any agreed-upon recommendations. It is important to stay proactive here. If an evaluation is moving slower than expected, make sure to assign additional resources to keep it on track.

These items should be on every agenda. If there is no update, that is fine, but it is important to keep bringing these things up so that they do not fall through the cracks. The Innovation Advocates can add additional items to the meetings as needed. Just be sure to keep the meetings short and to the point so that they remain a productive use of time.

Lastly, make sure to stick to the attendance requirements. The roles and responsibilities should provide clear expectations on attendance and the consequences for not adhering to them. If you let people get away without attending, you may one day find yourself hosting a meeting of one.

Resource: Innovation Meeting Agenda Template

The Innovation Meeting Agenda Template is a resource to help you run your innovation meetings. The core components that should be included on every Meeting Agenda are included in the template. Feel free to modify it, but make sure you are keeping your meetings productive.

Wrap-Up

We covered a lot in this section, and I hope you are still with me. This section should be used as a reference guide when creating your Innovation Strategy. Review this section often throughout the process, and print out the Innovation Strategy Framework graphic to help you along the way.

This graphic representation of the Innovation Strategy will help you clearly understand what lies ahead. Notice the order of the steps and refer to Section 5 for additional information. Take the time necessary to go through each of these steps, and commit to a specific time frame to accomplish each of them.

The important thing to remember is that you are not on this journey alone. The resources accompanying this book will get you well along your way, and the website, http://www.InnovationPACT.com, will be a great resource as you start taking action on your Innovation Strategy. Just take it one step at a time.

Section 4
Creating an Innovation Program

Innovation Programs have been mentioned frequently throughout this book, and now it is time to cover them in detail. Innovation is not something that can be easily controlled or focused. The Innovation Program is the primary tool we have to achieve that. It is the formal process of taking a problem, developing solutions, and implementing those solutions. We will cover all of these steps in detail shortly, but let's start by identifying when it is appropriate to use an Innovation Program.

The goal of this book is sustainable innovation, which usually requires small, incremental innovation that snowballs over time. The problem with the small-and-incremental approach is that many organizations are facing big problems that need to be resolved quickly. This is where a structured Innovation Program can come to the rescue.

You will also see Innovation Programs used heavily when trying to accomplish innovation through an external audience. The organization will reveal a problem to the external audience, and that audience will respond by presenting ideas. It will then be the responsibility of staff members to implement the most popular ideas. This can be a win–win because it allows your customers to become more connected to the organization and feel like they have a say in its overall direction.

Another common reason to create an Innovation Program is for innovation challenges. There may be times when you have not identified a problem or an inefficiency, but would like to just poll the organization or customers to see what ideas are out there. This type of challenge can be extremely beneficial and also extremely dangerous, so it should be managed carefully. If your external audience unanimously wants something that your organization is not willing to do, your innovation efforts can backfire.

For example, when the White House implemented its Ideation System, one of the most popular requests was to legalize marijuana. Legalizing a drug probably was not expected or something that could be easily implemented. I am guessing that the White House learned its lesson. It does not look good when you ask for input and, after you get it, you are unable to deliver.

The main problem with the White House's initial approach was that it did not create a challenge question. We will cover this in detail shortly, but it brings up an important point: What are the pros and cons of implementing a formal Innovation Program?

The pros have been covered throughout this book already and are pretty straightforward. A program can be focused, it can lead to big innovation quickly, and it allows you to get your external audience involved. The cons are that once you launch a program, you have to be accountable, you lose some control, and the results are not consistent.

That being said, Innovation Programs are still the most popular type of innovation initiatives organization implement, and that is one of my biggest motivators in writing this book. Innovation Programs are a worthy endeavor, but to create sustainable innovation you need an Innovation Strategy in place.

By taking this approach, the Innovation Program becomes another tool in your toolbox to help spark innovation. If you understand that, you will have great success. If you don't, you may find yourself on an innovation roller coaster.

Now that you understand how Innovation Programs should be used, you may be wondering how frequently you should be launching them. That is a great question. Innovation Programs require momentum to provide the best results. Therefore, you will need to do them frequently. The programs do not have to be stacked on top of one another, but do not go months between programs.

I recommend implementing a new Innovation Program within two to four weeks after the submission process is completed in the previous program. That will be frequent enough to keep momentum going and your audiences engaged.

Now let's look at what it takes to run an Innovation Program.

Figure 4a. Innovation Programs are broken down into six steps.

Creating a Challenge Question

One of the first things to do when creating an Innovation Strategy is to identify Organizational Pain Points. The Innovation Advocates will take one of the pain points and craft a question around it. This is your challenge question.

Creating challenge questions is not difficult, but it can be time-consuming. There is not a specific science behind it, and you will have to continuously tweak your questions and evaluate the results. However, I have a few tips to get you started, which will help point you in the right direction and give you a better chance of creating a challenge question that will get the results you want.

Review the Pain Point and Overarching Goal

During the pain-point-identification process, leadership will have identified the problem and the desired outcome. The more specific the pain point, the easier it will be to create a challenge question. Look at the key words used in both the problem and desired result. You do not want to be too specific in terms of results in your challenge question, but you want to make sure the question is focused enough that the responses will fit in with the desired results.

Don't Use Numbers

The challenge question should not include numbers or percentages. Numbers can constrain the responses you receive and also limit the number of responses. As it is difficult to quantify innovation, numbers can create unintentional barriers that get in the way of implementing a new idea.

Maintain Vagueness

I know that I stated that the question needs to be specific. However, challenge questions that are too specific limit innovative thinking. You want to focus on the problem area, not necessarily the specific problem. There may be ideas that completely eliminate the overarching process that is causing the problem. Allow people the opportunity to think bigger by not focusing your challenge question too narrowly.

Focus on Root Causes

A good pain-point-identification tactic will include looking at root causes, but that is not always the case. You may have to dig a little deeper to see exactly what is causing the problem. Focusing the question on those root causes can often provide better results than just focusing on the problem.

Provide Additional Information

Just because it's called a challenge question does not mean that it has to be limited to just a question. You can include an additional paragraph outlining why it is a problem and provide some history to help clarify.

Remember, not everyone will be as familiar with that problem as you are, so a little information can better equip your audience to provide a solution.

Use Easy-to-Understand Language

This may seem obvious, but try to avoid acronyms or any language that may be difficult to understand. Innovation can often be a collaborative effort, so someone does not have to be an expert to provide a good idea. A person's lack of knowledge in the problem area may enable him or her to submit something that others have not thought about. Your goal should be to open the doors to solutions that may not have been available otherwise.

Make It Personal

Make heavy use of the word "you" in your challenge questions: "What would *you* do?" instead of "What should *we* do?" This empowers your audience to share their opinion and ideas. It also puts the burden on them and provokes them to think deeply about how they would solve the challenge.

This simple mechanism provokes a more personal approach and gives your audience a chance to identify with the challenge. That will provide more meaningful comments since they aren't just solving some ethereal problem, but are providing a solution that can benefit them as well.

Challenge-Question Examples

Here are a couple of examples of good and bad challenge questions. I will focus on customer service and employee retention because those are areas every organization is familiar with.

Customer-Service Example

- Bad Question: "How can we increase our customer-service rating from 80 percent to 95 percent?"

- Good Question: "What changes would you make to improve the interactions we have with our customers?"

The bad question does not make it personal and makes leadership look like they only care about numbers. This does not provide much incentive for the audience to offer their opinions.

The good question gets in touch with the audience's thoughts and beliefs about customer service. It makes them think about what is truly best for the customer. Instead of being overly specific, it addresses the deeper problem: Do you want to improve the rating, or do you want to improve the relationship you have with your customers? There is no doubt that the relationship is more important and that the good question will provide better results.

Employee-Retention Example

- Bad Question: "What can we do to retain employees and attract talent?"

- Good Question: "What changes would you make that would increase your overall job satisfaction and make this an attractive place to work?"

The bad question in this scenario does not make it personal and does not focus on the root causes of the problem. The good question does. Attracting and retaining talent requires that you have satisfied workers and an attractive work environment. By focusing on those root causes, you will get more responses that address the deeper problem and will lead to better results.

Having a bad question may not make your Innovation Program a failure, but it won't produce the results that a good question would. A bad question can also lead to less effective responses and to ideas that sound good but do not really solve the problem. That is why it is important to make sure the question meets all of the criteria above. Do that, and you will be in good shape.

Gathering Ideas

You have crafted your challenge question and sent it out to the intended audience. Now it's time to gather the ideas. This process will look different depending on your Ideation System, but generally it is fairly hands-off. Just make sure you set a deadline and identify what information should be included in the responses. That way individuals know what they need to submit with their ideas and how much time they have to participate.

Submission Criteria

When you create a challenge question, you want to make sure the ideas submitted are as complete as possible. Think about the problem and what potential solutions might look like. Then you can craft the submission criteria accordingly. Each challenge question may be a little different, but here are some items to request when an idea is submitted.

- **Budget:** What does the submitter think it will cost to implement the idea? Will the solution have ongoing costs? This is great information to have during the selection process.

- **Impact:** What impact will the idea have on the organization? What impact will it have on current business processes or products? Considering these core concepts will help you see the overall value of the idea.

- **Examples:** Does the submitter know other departments or organizations that are doing something similar? If so, how has the idea helped that department or organization? By looking at real-world examples, you can get a better understanding of how the idea will impact your organization.

- **Stakeholders:** Who would be good to get involved in implementing the idea? How will the idea impact other employees or your external audience? This is important, because you can use this information to communicate the changes and get further input.

- **Deliverable:** What does the final product look like? How do you know when the idea is complete and functioning as intended? This information is helpful to provide you with a clear understanding of what project completion will look like.

- **Training:** What training will be required? How will people learn to operate when the new idea is in place? Change is difficult in most organizations, and training can help ensure that the changes are embraced.

These are just a few examples; I am sure you can identify more. Just be careful to ask only for information that is important to a specific innovation challenge. The submitter will do a lot of the legwork, but you do not want to make it so overwhelming that the person gives up.

Submission Time Frame

The time frame for submitting ideas should be long enough to give people an opportunity to do the necessary research, but short enough to promote a sense of urgency. In most situations, the size of the problem will directly relate to the length of the submission time frame. For smaller problems, give submitters only two weeks, but for more complex problems, consider giving them a month.

However, a month is the maximum amount of time I would consider. If you do not get a lot of traction, you can extend the time frame or re-launch the program by changing the marketing and possibly rephrasing the question.

Other Considerations

There are a few cautionary items to be aware of during this process. If you have Ideation software, you want to make sure someone is moderating it and removing inappropriate responses so they do not have an impact on the integrity of the system. Also, do your best to eliminate redundant ideas so that there is not too much clutter.

This period of the program is actually the fun part. Sit back and watch the creativity roll in. If things slow down, you can spark them back up by sending out additional communications or upping the ante, if that is an option. The goal is to keep the ideas coming in and the conversation flowing.

Idea Selection

If your idea-gathering process was a success, you will have a lot of ideas to sort through. There are different ways to approach this process, depending on if you are using Ideation software or a manual system. Let's take a look at each.

Ideation Software

If you have Ideation software, some of the work will have already been completed since the ideas are usually displayed to the audience as a whole. In this manner, Ideation software will allow individuals to discuss ideas more dynamically than a manual system. This means that ideas may already be fairly well hashed out, and if not, you can still go back to the software and continue the dialogue there.

Ideation software will usually have a ranking system built in. This means the ideas will already be prioritized for you. If the top-ranked ideas are viable options, your work is virtually complete. If the idea is not viable but was popular, you need to make sure to provide feedback as to why it was not considered. This is crucial because you do not want to undermine the ranking system.

The next step depends on your process for selecting ideas. In most cases, the best submissions will be reviewed by a team of top organizational leaders. The person who submitted the idea may be brought in to answer questions and present the idea. This team will make the ultimate selection on which idea or ideas are going to be implemented.

Manual System

Ideas submitted through a manual system will most likely need a little work. The Innovation Advocacy team will have to review the submitted ideas and consolidate them into a list so that they can be ranked. If this process is handled entirely by the Innovation Advocacy team, then the filtering, ranking, and selection may all be combined into a single exercise.

Once the ideas have been filtered to a select few, you will move to the next step. Similar to the formal process, this is where leadership will select the idea or ideas that are going to be implemented.

Participation Feedback

To maintain the integrity of the Ideation System and keep participation high, you will want to make sure you provide as much feedback as possible. It may be too time-consuming to write individual responses to every submitter, but you should always explain why an idea was selected over the others. This includes the good and the bad.

Through feedback, you are also training participants on how the system should be used and what you are looking for. If individuals submitting ideas never get any feedback, they might think their ideas were insignificant or overlooked and choose not to participate in the future. They may even write the entire system off as rigged or pointless. It is important to make sure this does not happen.

Implementing the Idea

You have a great idea in hand, and now you are ready to make it happen. The implementation phase is exciting as this is when all of your hard work comes to fruition. This process will be handled in a unique way by each organization.

Sometimes you will be lucky enough to be in a situation where the person who submitted the idea is also capable of implementing it. That is great. However, in many situations this will not be the case. Therefore, implementing an idea should be turned over to the most capable people you have.

The biggest caveat with any idea is that you want to make sure to maintain its integrity. People have a way of making things their own, and that may not always be the best move. To prevent this, you should include one of the Innovation Advocates as a stakeholder on the project. That person should be kept in the loop to make sure the outcome closely resembles the initial idea.

The Innovation Advocate will also get to see the impact of the idea, which will help prepare him or her for future projects. This will be great feedback in the Innovation Program Review. It will allow him or her to seek additional resources if there are any roadblocks and ensure everything stays on track. This is important to make sure you are getting the full value out of your Innovation Program.

Program Review

Going through the entire process from challenge question to implementation is a lot of work. It will not always be perfect, and there will be learning opportunities. That is where the Program Review comes in.

During the review process, you should include the person who submitted the idea, the Innovation Advocacy team, and the person in charge of implementing the idea. You may also want to liaise with the leadership involved in selecting the idea. Discuss the good and the bad of the entire process, and look for ways to improve for next time. As with all meetings, make sure someone is taking notes.

During this process you will also want to document the success story. Gather success stories every chance you get, because not every program will run smoothly. It is a good idea to review the successes and the failures prior to your next program. That way you can continue to learn from the process. If you keep getting better, your Innovation Programs will have a higher likelihood of success in the future.

Celebration

It is time to celebrate! You have just implemented new innovation within your organization, and this should not be taken lightly. Think of all the people involved in making it happen. It is quite a feat.

Make sure you take the time to recognize your innovators. This does not have to involve a formal public ceremony, but you should do something. You can hold an annual recognition event, provide some type of monetary award, or put your own spin on it and do something creative. Just do it!

Wrap-Up

Creating an Innovation Program is something that you will get better at over time. The information in this section provided you with a big head start and will help you avoid some of the common mistakes many organizations make. Work your way through each step and adjust as you gain experience. Here is a simple breakdown of each step that you can refer to throughout the process.

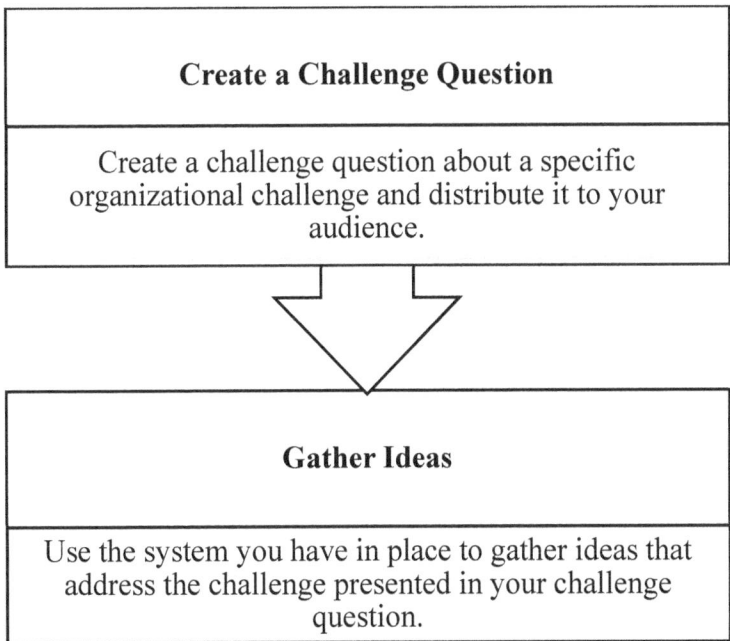

Create a Challenge Question

Create a challenge question about a specific organizational challenge and distribute it to your audience.

Gather Ideas

Use the system you have in place to gather ideas that address the challenge presented in your challenge question.

Select the Best Ideas

Review the submitted ideas by combining similar ideas and ranking them. The best idea or ideas should move on to implementation.

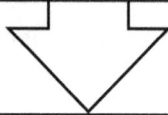

Implement the Idea

Work with the necessary stakeholders and organizational units to gather the required resources and then implement the idea.

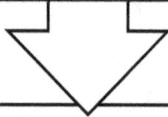

Review the Process

Take the time necessary to review each Innovation Program for development and learning opportunities.

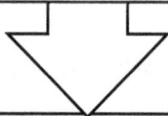

Celebrate your Successes

Take the time to celebrate your successes. Implementing an Innovation Program requires people working together, and this should be recognized.

The Innovation Program is a great tool for achieving innovation within your organization. If you use it alongside other initiatives covered in the Innovation Strategy, you will see results. Now it is time to put everything we have learned so far into action. The next section provides a step-by-step walkthrough for implementing your Innovation Strategy.

Section 5

Implementing Your Innovation Strategy

Now it's time to implement your Innovation Strategy. I am going to assume that you will be using the resources provided, but they are not required to complete this section.

This step-by-step guide will be your ultimate source for bringing all of the information and other resources together. If you follow these steps, you will have a completed Innovation Strategy by the time we are done. There is no need to read this section until you are ready to start creating your Innovation Strategy. Feel free to skip ahead to section 6 if you are not ready to start at this time.

Before we get started, let's take a look at all of the resources available. All of these are available at the Innovation PACT website, and additional resources will become available there as needs are identified. Start by downloading all of the resources so that you have them in one place, and then work through the steps in this section. It will be an exciting journey, and I hope you will share your experience on the website once you are done.

Resources

Innovation Meeting Agenda Template

This is a sample agenda that includes all of the standard items that should be included in every innovation meeting.

Innovation Officer Job Description

This outlines the core roles and responsibilities that should be included when hiring an Innovation Officer.

Innovation PACT Graphic

The graphic is a visual representation of the Innovation PACT.

Innovation Programs List Template

This spreadsheet can be used to keep track of your completed, active, and future Innovation Programs.

Innovation Strategy Framework

This is a graphical representation of the core components and the process to create an Innovation Strategy.

Innovation Strategy Template

This template, which will be your starting point, covers all of the core components of the Innovation Strategy.

Innovation Team Roles and Responsibilities

This sheet outlines the core roles and responsibilities that should govern the Innovation Advocacy team.

Innovation Training Plan Template

This spreadsheet can be used to track all innovation training and associated costs.

Leading Innovation Presentation

This presentation provides an overview of the topics discussed in this book in a format that can be presented to leadership.

Policy Review List Template

This spreadsheet can be used to track your completed, active, and future policies to be reviewed.

Process Evaluation List Template

This spreadsheet can be used to keep track of your completed, active, and future processes to be evaluated.

Step-by-Step Instructions

Now we will walk through all of the steps required to create your Innovation Strategy. Each step will include the resource name and the section where the topic was covered in this book. Note that the steps will not outline all the details required to complete them; you will have to refer back to the specific section to get more information. This is just a simple list to make it easier to use the information presented here.

You will also notice an "assigned to" section under each step. This information will help identify who will be responsible for completing the step. These are best practices, but if you feel that someone else should be involved or oversee the responsibility of making sure the step is completed, that is your call. The important thing is to make sure that it gets done and that the appropriate stakeholders are involved.

I am going to assume you have already read the book up to this point; that is obviously the first step. Follow the steps one by one, and take the time necessary to complete each one before moving to the next. Let's get started.

Step 1: Leading Innovation Presentation

Use the Leading Innovation Presentation to present the topics covered in this book to your leadership team. An initiative as big as this should be discussed among your entire leadership team.

Assigned to: Person in charge of implementing the Innovation Strategy

Resource: Leading Innovation Presentation

Step 2: Innovation Goals

Now that you have leadership on board, start working on the Innovation Goals. Go through the process of identifying the three to five main reasons your organization is looking to be more innovative. Once completed, add the Innovation Goals to the strategy document.

Assigned to: Leadership

Resources: Innovation Strategy Template

Section: Section 3, Innovation Goals

Step 3: Organizational Pain Points

Now that you have completed your Innovation Goals, identify two to three pain points under each goal. This can be accomplished through a brainstorming session or a formal process. Once completed, add the Organizational Pain Points to the strategy document.

Assigned to: Leadership

Resources: Innovation Strategy Template

Section: Section 3, Organizational Pain Points

Step 4: Innovation PACT (Optional)

The Innovation PACT section is completed for you, but if you would like to add your own initiatives or make any changes, feel free to do so. Any changes you make should be updated in this section of the Innovation Strategy.

Assigned to: Leadership

Resources: Innovation Strategy Template, Innovation PACT Graphic

Section: Section 3, Innovation PACT

Step 5: Lead Innovation Advocate

Now that you have the high-level goals and pain points identified, it is time to recruit some help. If you are going to hire, now is the time to start looking. If you are recruiting internally, look for someone with great communication and leadership skills.

Assigned to: Leadership

Resources: Innovation Officer Job Description

Section: Section 3, Advocacy

Step 6: Innovation Advocacy Team (Optional)

Once you have a Lead Innovation Advocate, he or she will need to start putting together a team. If you are not using the team approach, you can skip this step, but it is highly recommended that you use some sort of team for sustainability. Once the team is assembled, it will need to conduct its first meeting and finalize its roles and responsibilities. Once completed, be sure to update the Innovation Strategy.

Assigned to: Lead Innovation Advocate

Resources: Innovation Strategy Template, Innovation Team Roles and Responsibilities, Innovation Meeting Agenda Template

Section: Section 3, Advocacy

Step 7: Ideation System

Innovation Programs will be a big part of the Innovation Strategy, and this is where you define what that formal innovation process will look like. Use the information in the Ideation System section to complete this step and then add it to Innovation Strategy.

Assigned to: Innovation Advocates

Resources: Innovation Strategy Template

Section: Section 3, Ideation System

Step 8: Ideation Software (Optional)

If you choose to use software to manage your Ideation System, you will need to select it now. Make sure the software is a good fit for your organization. (If you are doing a manual Ideation System, you can skip this step.) Once completed, be sure to add the Ideation software information to the Innovation Strategy.

Assigned to: Innovation Advocates

Resources: Innovation Strategy Template

Section: Section 3, Ideation System

Step 9: Working Documents

Completing the Working Documents can be done simultaneously. Although they do not have to be perfect at this point, it is a good idea to start filling them out. This includes the Innovation Programs, Process Evaluations, Policy Reviews, and Training Plan. These documents are referenced in the Innovation Strategy but do not reside there because they are frequently updated. They should instead be placed in a location that all of the Innovation Advocates have access to.

Assigned to: Innovation Advocates

Resources: Innovation Programs List Template, Policy Review List Template, Process Evaluation List Template, Innovation Training Plan Template

Section: Section 3, Innovation Strategy Working Documents

Step 10: Innovation Budget

After selecting the Ideation software (if applicable) and completing the Innovation Training Plan, you should have a good idea of your expenses. Determine where the funds will come from and complete the current year budget. Information on how innovation will be funded and purchasing authority should be added to the Innovation Strategy. The actual line-item budget can go in the financial system you currently have in place.

Assigned to: Innovation Advocates, Finance

Resources: Innovation Strategy Template

Section: Section 3, Budget

Step 11: Personalize

This book presents just the core components. If you want to customize the document and add additional sections, feel free to do so. At this time you can also add your own branding, letterhead, and/or customized fonts and layouts. Make the document represent your organization.

Assigned to: Innovation Advocates

Resources: Innovation Strategy Template

Step 12: Executive Summary

Once you have completed all of the components of the Innovation Strategy, it is time to write the Executive Summary. This should summarize the document and provide some guidance on how it is structured. Once completed, add this as the first page of the Innovation Strategy.

Assigned to: Innovation Advocates, Leadership

Resources: Innovation Strategy Template

Section: Section 3, Executive Summary

Step 13: First Innovation Program

You should have already identified some potential Innovation Programs, and now it is time to launch the first one. This will require defining the target audience, setting the time frame, creating your challenge question, and preparing any promotional material. I would highly recommend that you try the program internally first before going external. This will help you get the hang of it before too many people are watching.

Assigned to: Innovation Advocates, Leadership

Section: Section 3, Innovation Programs

Step 14: Training

It is a good idea to time any training and the launch of your first Innovation Program closely together. You can even use the training as a promotional tool. You should provide training on the Ideation System, Ideation software (if applicable), and some high-level innovation topics. Make sure the training is included in your Innovation Training Plan.

Assigned to: Innovation Advocates

Resources: Innovation Strategy Template

Section: Section 3, Executive Summary

Step 15: Ready...Set...Go!

You are now ready to get rolling with your Innovation Strategy. It is important that you complete all of the aforementioned components before going forward. It is also important that the Innovation Advocates are meeting regularly so that they can keep things moving and ensure that leadership is informed on all of the initiatives.

Your innovation journey has now officially begun! That is great and it should be celebrated, but the fun is not over.

In the next section, we will cover maintaining the Innovation Strategy. This is how you will continuously adapt and maintain your strategy so that you continue to get great results for many years to come. Congratulations! If you get a chance, please visit the website and share your experience.

Wrap-Up

You are now rolling with your Innovation Strategy, and shortly you will begin to see innovation trickling in. You are ahead of the majority of organizations, and that is a great place to be when it comes to innovation.

Just remember the first letter of the Innovation PACT as you go through this process. Persistence is key, and your innovation efforts will take a little time to pay off. Stick with it!

Section 6

Maintaining Your Innovation Strategy

The hard work is in the rearview mirror, but do not let off the gas just yet. You may have a completed Innovation Strategy, but it will require some maintenance for it to be successful. The good news is that maintaining your strategy is a fairly light job. In this section, we will take a look at exactly what that entails.

Innovation Strategy Core Components

Maintaining the Innovation Strategy will require a formal review at least once a year. You want to make sure that the goals and pain points are updated and that any changes to the Ideation System or advocacy team are also documented.

Similar to the original creation of the document, leadership should be involved. Organizational leaders do not have to do all of the work, but they need to be involved at some point during the review process—most likely during the review of the goals and pain points. This will ensure that the strategy stays in alignment with the overall vision of leadership.

Let's take a look at each component and see what it takes to maintain it.

Goals and Pain Points

As with the creation of the Innovation Strategy, you want to be sure to review the goals and pain points first. This will keep the rest of the strategy consistent with the overall goals. All changes should be approved by leadership and then updated in the Innovation Strategy.

Start by reviewing the goals. Have any of the goals been achieved or dropped in priority? Has a new priority been identified? If the answer to either of these questions is yes, then you need to update the Innovation Strategy. Also, if there have been many changes in organizational leadership, it may be beneficial to start from scratch. Doing so will ensure that everyone is on board with the priorities.

Once you have completed the goals, take a look at pain points. Chances are that you will have completed a number of Innovation Programs, and some of the pain points may have improved or been completely eliminated. Be sure to remove any pain points that are not a priority anymore and add any new ones. A good rule of thumb is to have at least two pain points under each goal.

Ideation System

During the review process, you may also want to review the Ideation System and software. It is important to make sure that the Ideation System is functioning efficiently. The goal is to promote innovation, but if the system itself is not running efficiently, it can serve as a roadblock.

The best place to look is at the feedback received during the Innovation Program Reviews. If there were any delays, misunderstandings, or unnecessary work, they should be evaluated for improvements.

Advocacy

When it comes to advocacy, the Innovation Advocates' roles and responsibilities should be reviewed, including how the team or individual is handling the workload. Start by having the Innovation Advocates review their roles and responsibilities to make sure they still match what the advocates are actually doing. If not, make the necessary changes or have them refrain from doing any unnecessary work.

This is also a great opportunity to assign additional responsibilities, if needed. The goal is to maintain a clear understanding of what the Innovation Advocates' roles and responsibilities are. That way, they are continuously working on the right things.

Lastly, take a look at their workload and team dynamics. Make sure the workload is balanced and not overwhelming or underwhelming. If some of the team members are not performing, it may be a good time to recruit new members. Make sure the Innovation Advocacy Team is functioning at a high level.

Working Documents

The Working Documents are just that: *working* documents. That means they should be updated regularly and reviewed constantly. This will be one of the responsibilities of the Innovation Advocates and should happen at least once a month. If you have an Innovation Advocacy team in place, it should be meeting at least monthly to take care of this. Let's take a look at each of the documents and how they should be updated.

Innovation Programs List

The Innovation Programs List should reflect the status of all of your Innovation Programs. This should be a snapshot of everything going on, which means it should be updated as Innovation Programs move through the process. It is a good idea to schedule innovation meetings around the time an Innovation Program progresses to the next step. There is probably some action the Innovation Advocates have to take at this point, and handling that as a group is usually the best.

Maintaining the Innovation Programs List will include the following:

- Archiving completed Innovation Programs

- Updating status of active Innovation Programs

- Adding or removing Innovation Programs

Share the updated list with leadership quarterly, as it is critical to have everyone on the same page so you can keep the programs moving forward.

Policy Review List

The Policy Review List should be updated at the regular innovation meetings or maintained by the Innovation Officer. Policy reviews should be delegated to individual Innovation Advocates so that they have access to and are able to make the updates to the document. The updates should be reviewed at innovation meetings to make sure the policy review process is staying on track.

It is a good idea to keep leadership and HR up-to-date on the Policy Review List. The Innovation Advocates will most likely not have any authority to change policies, but they should be charged with making recommendations. In most organizations, these recommendations will be reviewed by HR at a minimum and may need leadership support to get approved.

Maintaining the Policy Review List will include the following:

- Marking policy reviews as complete

- Updating the status of active policy reviews

- Adding new policies to review

- Reviewing recommended changes to policies

The Lead Innovation Advocate needs to make sure the recommendations get to the right people for review. This process should be set up in a way that makes sense for the organization. As long as the reviews are taking place and beneficial changes are being considered, you are doing your part.

Process Evaluation List

The Process Evaluation List is usually updated less frequently than the other two lists. Like the other lists, though, it should be reviewed in the regular innovation meetings. There may also be additional information that will need to be presented at meetings to keep everyone informed.

Maintaining the Process Evaluation List will include the following:

- Marking process evaluations as complete

- Updating the status of active process evaluations

- Adding additional processes to evaluate

- Making recommendations to improve a reviewed process

These updates should be shared at a minimum with the business unit in charge of the process, and in some situations they may also need to be reviewed by leadership. This will keep all of the appropriate people informed of the status of the evaluation.

Be sure to keep a close eye on the process evaluations. The long time frame and multiple stakeholders involved can make them more susceptible to missed deadlines and low-quality deliverables. During the monthly innovation meetings, it is important to stay on top of these documents and catch any delays as early as possible. Look for common procrastination techniques, and ask for details when getting an update. Stay on top of it and hold people accountable. This will make your process evaluations successful.

Innovation Training Plan

The Innovation Training Plan is not as straightforward as the other living/working documents. The goal here is to identify as much training as early as possible and also to account for any last-minute training. Make sure you keep providing training so that innovation stays at the front of everyone's mind.

The Lead Innovation Advocate should review the Training Plan at every meeting unless there is absolutely nothing to talk about. Innovation Advocates should be adding their training to the plan and identifying new training opportunities for the organization and external audiences. Capture all innovation training, no matter who the audience is and when it happened. This includes any publications, in-person training, webinars, and books that are read by the group.

The reason it is so important to maintain an Innovation Training Plan is because this will serve as both a reference and a planning tool. Review it around budget time to help plan for the following year's budget and also to get ideas on future training topics. This document will serve as a great resource and should not be overlooked.

Budget

Most organizations have some type of formal budgeting process in place, so this will be fairly obvious. Funds allocated to innovation may come from a variety of sources, so it is important to keep an eye out for what they are being spent on.

The first year may be a shot in the dark, but after that you should have some real data to help justify and allocate the funds. The Training Plan, software costs, and innovation-team expenses should not fluctuate much from year to year. As with any new initiative, things tend to increase in cost over time, but don't be afraid to put financial constraints in place. Sometimes that can be a great tool to promote innovation.

Ideation Software

If you are using software to manage your Ideation System, you need to make sure the software is meeting your needs. Usability, functionality, and administration of the system can have a huge impact on the success of your Innovation Programs. Therefore, it is important to make sure you have the right software in place and that you are getting everything you were promised.

Feedback on the Ideation software may not be as easy to gather. Listen to what people are saying. Are they having trouble using the software? Is the functionality meeting your needs? Is managing the Innovation Programs relatively simple? Is the software being used to its full capabilities? Is the software a good value for the cost? These are all questions you need to ask to make sure you have the right software.

Even if you are getting some negative answers to the previous questions, keep in mind that no software is exactly perfect for every organization. You will have to decide if the problems are significant enough to start over with something new. Sometimes with a software migration, additional training may be required or additional features may need to be set up. Be sure to look at the complete picture before making a decision. If you take all of these aspects into consideration, the right choice should be fairly clear.

Staying Persistent

Maintaining your Innovation Strategy may seem like a lot of work, but if done properly, it can provide a huge return on investment. Rely heavily on your innovation team or Innovation Officer to complete the majority of the work, as that is what they are there for. This will prevent any delays caused by the excessive workload placed on leadership.

Make sure your innovation team is meeting monthly and that you are reviewing the Innovation Strategy annually at a minimum. Not doing so can lead to missed opportunities and can result in the entire initiative fizzling out. Chances are you have put a lot of hard work into getting your Innovation Strategy off the ground, so please make the effort to keep it going.

Conclusion

It is time to take everything you have learned and put it into action. You are well on your way to becoming more innovative, and that is exciting. I hope you have found the information presented useful and will strongly consider the resources as you proceed on this journey. Before you get started, let's do a short recap so that you know exactly what lies ahead.

Foundation

As stated at the beginning, this is not a book about the science of innovation; it is intended to be action based. The number-one goal is to help you create sustainable innovation inside your organization. With that being said, it is still important to understand the concepts in Section 1.

Start by making sure your definition of innovation matches the definition outlined in this book:

> *Innovation is the introduction of new ways to handle situations or problems that provide a better result than the current methods.*

This will ensure that we are all on the same page as you work through the Innovation Strategy process.

Additionally, two important concepts to be gathered from this book are Ideation and Ideation Systems. Ideation is the process of generating ideas and can be easily remembered by blending the words "idea" and "generation." An Ideation System is a formal system for Ideation. The system works by identifying specific problems and enlisting individuals who then submit ideas to solve that problem. Once possible solutions have been generated, these ideas are ranked, and finally one or more should be selected.

Lastly, you need to make sure you understand the different types of innovation, or the four *C*s of innovation: Creative Innovation, Continuous Innovation, Collaborative Innovation, and Captivating Innovation. All types of innovation are important, but organizations should focus on Continuous and Collaborative Innovation for sustainable innovation.

Innovation PACT

Leading innovation requires that you really take a look at your organization and make sure the right components are in place. Certain things are required for innovation to flourish. The Innovation PACT graphic below sums it up, but leadership must identify the areas that need improvement and put in the work.

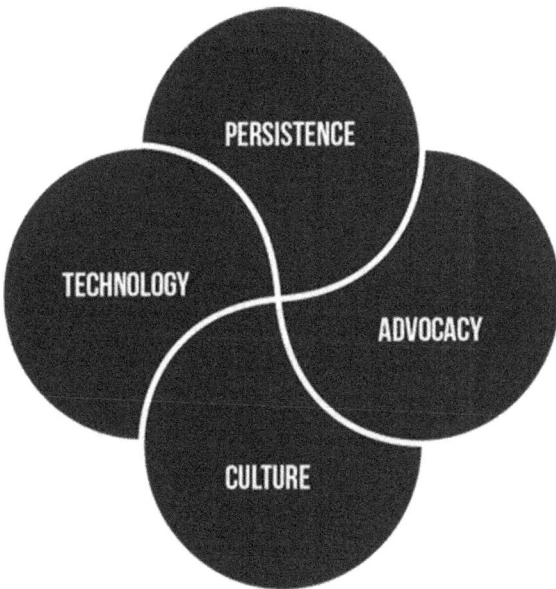

With persistence, you will overcome most obstacles, and you are not in it alone. The Innovation Advocates will play a crucial role in promoting innovation throughout your organization. To do this they need to be enabled by leadership, and a supportive culture must be developed. Then you can look to technology to solve some of your biggest challenges.

Always remember that change is difficult for some people. Many great initiatives fail because of an inability to get other people to change. By taking an incremental approach to change, you can build the level of comfort over time. This requires that you take the time to build the culture and develop a good team of Innovation Advocates. Doing these things will greatly improve your chances for success.

Innovation Strategy

Creating an Innovation Strategy might be one of the easiest initiatives you will ever undertake. It can also be easy to execute if you take the advice in this book and put the right people in charge. In this book, we covered the core components of the Innovation Strategy and provided you with a framework that will help you get through the process.

Take the time to go through each of the components and follow the guidance provided in Section 3. Download all of the resources from http://www.InnovationPACT.com and start knocking them out. Refer back to Section 5 for a step-by-step guide. This is an exciting process, and the benefits of executing your Innovation Strategy can be very rewarding.

Final Thoughts…

There are many ways to increase innovation within an organization. The process outlined in this book is what I have seen work and have direct experience with. It is also the simplest model I have come across for increasing innovation.

As you get further along in your innovation efforts, you may decide to include ideas and components from other systems. That is great! This book is a starting point and is designed to be flexible so that all organizations can benefit. The most important thing is to get started, and then constantly evaluate your progress and look for improvements.

Thank you for taking the time to read *Innovation PACT*. Be sure to check out http://www.InnovationPACT.com for the latest information and resources.

Creativity is just connecting things. When you ask creative people how they did something, they feel a little guilty because they didn't really do it, they just saw something. It seemed obvious to them after a while. That's because they were able to connect experiences they've had and synthesize new things. And the reason they were able to do that was that they've had more experiences or they have thought more about their experiences than other people.

—Steve Jobs